T0067916

BREACH OF
CONTRACT

What the Government doesn't want you to know

Bradley J. Franks & Robert C. Simpson

authorHOUSE®

AuthorHouse™
1663 Liberty Drive
Bloomington, IN 47403
www.authorhouse.com
Phone: 833-262-8899

Published by AuthorHouse 12/16/2022

ISBN: 978-1-6655-7837-0 (sc)
ISBN: 978-1-6655-7836-3 (e)

Library of Congress Control Number: 2022923291

Print information available on the last page.

This book is printed on acid-free paper.

CONTENTS

Dedication...vii
Acknowledgments..ix

Chapter 1: Action And Reaction.. 1
Chapter 2: Types of Contracts...17
Chapter 3: "Breach Of Contract".. 36
Chapter 4: A Remedy For "Breach Of Contract"
           With Examples From Politicians 82
Chapter 5: The Author's Last Word................................... 270
Chapter 6: Glossary Of Terminology And Definitions 278

DEDICATION

This book is dedicated for all those Americans that are very much aware that the Immediate United States Corporate Government and its subsidiaries are committing crimes against its civilians in the name of "It's just a Job" and to stuff their bank accounts.

Hopefully this book along with the other two will help enlighten those that need help against such heinous crimes against them.

We wish to further dedicate this book for all American-Civilians that are aware that the UNITED STATES-Corporate-Government is "Broken" and needs to be fixed before we lose what our "Forefathers established". The UNITED STATES-Corporate-Government seeks to indenture, enslave or imprison ANY American-Civilian who speaks out against the "crooked-corrupt" establishment either verbally or within written truth and facts. They will use "Biased-Opinionated-Perjury" through the News Media and through their carefully controlled Court System.

ACKNOWLEDGMENTS

We wish to acknowledge all parties that through their work, help, research and information this book would not be possible. In addition, we want to thank the greedy corrupt Political-Corporate-Whores and the Judicial 'morons' who take us for 'idiots' and ignorant and are under the impression they can do whatever they want-to-anyone they want-anytime they want.

Furthermore, we wish to acknowledge and thank all of the Secretary of States for doing their duty in sending copies of the elected officials "contracts" also known as the "Oath/Affirmation", without their fastidiousness, diligence and research this book would not come into existence.

Chapter 1

ACTION AND REACTION

ENCOUNTERS OF THE EVIL KIND: from 1983 – 2017

We start this book with a brief history as a reminder of what took place from **1983 – 2017** through our decisions/actions (wrong or right) and what the Subsidiary-Corporate-Government of the STATE OF CALIFORNIA, its Politicians/ Judicial Officers/Agents; Agents/Officers, Bureaucrats/ Employees and anyone else (known or unknown) who was directly and/or indirectly involved with "Breach of Contract", "Racketeer Influenced and Corrupt Organization" laws and "Money Laundering". The following information is taken directly out of "! AT GUN POINT... Whistle Blowers' Point of View" Published through Author House **04/19/2012**. Authors Bradley – J.: [Franks] and Robert – C.: [Simpson].

    1983 - Robert – Charles: [Simpson] begins construction of his home located in California State, County of Riverside, in an unincorporated area called Thousand Palms. We used our own labor, time and finances under what was known at that time as; "Owner-Builder".

    Robert and I went to the "Building and Safety"; located in Indio, seeking information concerned with which if any "Laws" we would or could be in violation of if we build our home "without" permits (known to some as extortion-money). An Inspector by the name of "McLeod" (last name only) stated, "None. However, the County will not allow the electric company to hook up the electricity". (At the time the Electric Company was Imperial Irrigation Water and Power. A county owned and controlled business). McLeod further explained that "It was our Right to build our home as Owner-Builder". In reality we did not mind if we were not allowed an electrical hook-up, because we decided to go with an alternative electrical source (i. e. generator, wind power and solar power).

We then asked about Size-variances. Was there a 'minimum' square footage? McLeod stated, "Yes, a minimum of 750 square feet. However, there is no maximum for the square footage." Robert and I asked one-more question about Height-variance. The answer McLeod stated was that "there is no height-variance." McLeod then physically wrote down (pen to paper) the measurements that we were able to build by, they were/are as follows: "10' from the back property-line; 5' on each side of the property-line; and 27 ½' from the center of the Street". However we went 29' from the center of the street.

The County Supervisor for the Fourth District Riverside County, at the time, was Al McCandles.

After time went by, a new administration was elected into the County Supervisor's Office. That is when our problems really began. Out of Malicious Intent, Hatred, Spite and Jealousy, the new administration moved against us for following the above stated "information" that was given to us by 'McLeod'.

1989 – Robert obtained the finances to pay-off the balance of the mortgage and was instructed by an Attorney by the name of Stephen L. Fingal NOT to "Record the Variance with Riverside County".

This was the same year I decided to see if I could make a difference in helping Americans for injustices I witnessed by Campaigning for County Supervisor and Campaigning against an Incumbent who was extremely crooked, prejudiced and corrupt...and proved it.

1990 – 1992 – Robert and I continued to build our home without interruption. However Robert decided to Campaign for Congress in 1991 against Al McCandles but did not pass the Primaries.

1993 – I once again decided to Campaign for County Supervisor for Riverside County Fourth District and Campaign for Change on massive scale. But once again I was defeated by the powers that be that are in control of Riverside County and the State of California legally or illegally.

1994 – I started a business that was set up to help the customers of the "Electric-Companies" from information I received during the Campaign. The Billing process of the electric companies across the nation are sending out fraudulent bills by claiming that they are "measuring the consumption" between $300.00+ and $700.00+ dollars-worth of electricity per month, just for residential zones alone.

1995 – 1996 - Robert and I continued to expose the electric companies and reported this crime too Senator Barbara Levy Boxer; Assemblyman James F. Battin; Public Utility Commissioner of California Josiah Nepier; Federal Energy Regulatory Commission; which turned out to be Bill Richardson appointed by the Clinton Administration before becoming Governor of New Mexico; Internal Revenue Service; Riverside County Supervisor Roy Wilson and all of the Mayors and City Counsels surrounding Palm Springs. We also reported and interviewed by the "Desert Sun" **August 21, 1996** written by: Cecelia Chan. We were also guests on talk-radio programs (Ron Fortner, Art Bell and Chuck Harder) explaining how the electric companies were defrauding their customers. In the interim of all of this, the Electric Companies finally admitted that "Yes they can

3

speed-up or slow-down the meter. But trust us we would never commit fraud".

1997 – 2001 – I came to the decision to ask Supervisor Roy Wilson "what laws would I be breaking if I staged a Peaceful Protest" against the Electric Companies? Mr. Wilson's reply was as follows, "None. It is within your rights as an American too 'protest' against illegal-acts against Americans".

So on **August 04, 1997** I climbed a "Utility-Pole" NOT the 'Power-Pole', that belonged to Robert – C. Simpson and sat on the cross-piece where the Phone-Line and Television Cable connect for their services. Robert was arrested and charged with "Theft Utility Services" for Twenty-Years and "Obtain Utility w/out Paying". I was charged with "Theft Utility Services" for Twenty-Years; "Obtain Utility W/out Paying"; "Resisting Arrest"; "Trespass/Refuse to leave land"; and "Obstruction of Justice".

On **March 24, 1998** - Robert and I were found "Guilty" on certain counts. However, the jury at the time found and declared us "NOT GUILTY". The judge at the time 'refused' the verdict and instructed the jury to "re-deliberate the case and come to a DIFFERENT verdict or they would be sequestered for as long as it took to change their decision".

On **May 1, 1998** - Robert and I were once again 'ordered' for Report and Sentencing before the court. We were terrified that were going to be sentenced for up to 25 years in prison for a crime that according to the County of Riverside never took place. But as luck would have it, all we received was 15 days of community-service with a Jewish Owned and Jewish Mafia Controlled business called "The Palm Spring Desert Air Museum" and "restitution" for crimes that were not committed.

In **1999 – 2000** - we resided within our home continuing the construction hoping that this would be the end of the punishment for exposing a crime against Americans.

In **2001** – Governor Gray Davis demanded 9 Billion U. S.

Dollars refund for the "Power Overcharges", in an article from the "Desert Sun" dated: **June 21, 2001**; written by H. Josef Herbert.

In **December 2, 2001** came the downfall of Enron. We were known as the "outside-source". The subsidiary in Texas was the focal point of Money-Laundering for the State of California for their Retirement, Pension Funds and 'Slush Funds' for all of the Employees of the Corporate Government of California and the 'Politicians'. When California, realized the truth in what we reported as a crime, they withdrew all of the 'finances' it invested within Enron, which helped in the cause of the Collapse of the Texas based subsidiary. In reality, the State of California was Laundering-Money for their selfish greed and got caught.

Robert and I were "Ordered" by Senator Barbara Levy Boxer through all of the County Agents/Employees, Police, and the Court system to "Get out of California or you will die". The exact quote was "We want their home gone, his son gone, and Robert gone and not necessarily in that order".

Our home was demolished and the land sold for "Back-Taxes"; with an added charge of $265,000 dollars for the demolition; of which they applied through a Lien. Our taxes were paid up until **1998**, and yes we still have that "Original" documentation; Tax-receipts, that the courts and all known an unknown perpetrators refused to 'notice' as evidence.

According to the Laws of California and their Tax-Laws a person has 5 years to catch up their property taxes. Furthermore, before any person can pay their "current" Property-Taxes they have to pay for the arrears-taxes (taxes they are behind on). Our property-taxes were current as of **1998**, with the documentation (receipts from the tax assessor's office).

However, we were forced to become homeless and traveled until 2002.

The following information is taken directly from "Your

Day In Court" Using Common Law With Common Sense";
Published through Lulu Publishing Company in 2011; Authors;
Bradley J. Franks and Robert – C. Simpson.

In **2002 – 2006** - I applied for a career as a 'Correction
Officer' in Torrance County, New Mexico. However, what
we did not realize, until it was almost too late, was that Bill
Richardson (appointed to be in charge of the Federal Energy
Regulatory Commission by the Clinton Administration)
became the Governor of New Mexico, at this time.

I purchased a 5-acre parcel of property with permanent-
mobile-home with add-ons, septic system and a private-
well. The entire mortgage was complete and paid-off on
November 4, 2005.

Robert decided to help protect the residential structure
by building a 'Pole-Building-Structure" around the existing-
trailer for protection from hail and other weather conditions;
including screened-in-porches. We contacted a State
Building Code Enforcement Officer by the name of Fema
Aragon. We asked if there were any "permits" required for
a "Pole-Building" in the State of New Mexico. His reply was
"No. For a Pole-Building there are no-permits required".

In **March 21, 2006** - I decided to try and Campaign
one more time to help Americans that were in need of
help from those Crooked Corrupt Bureaucrats/Employees/
Agents/Officers/Elected or Appointed Officials that were in
the practice of using T. D. C. (Threat, Duress and Coercion).
I Campaigned for Magistrate of Torrance County against
the "Incumbent; Steve Jones 'also known as Larry Jones'".
Unfortunately, some of the "polling-sites were closed" or
the "Democrats did not vote"; either way I was not elected
and furthermore, the Secretary of State of New Mexico did
not "Sanction" the election during that time at the County
level.

In **May 21, 2007** - I received a "criminal complaint", (that
any reasonable-intelligent-individual would observe that
was "false" upon its face). The charges were as follows: "1

count of Solid Waste, 1 count of Public Nuisance, 1 count Development Review Permit, 1 count of Abandonment of Dangerous Containers." The description is as follows: "1 accumulation of trash, C&D materials and appliances on the property; 2 the addition to the mobile home on the property with no land use permit; 3 you notified back in May 2007 as to the need of the cleanup of the property and to obtain a land use permit were given time to do so". The complaint was autographed by Richard A. Ledbetter.

The agent/officer who autographed the "complaint" also claimed he was the "prosecution" and "decision-maker" of this case, in other words he appointed himself as judge, jury and executioner. He was nothing but an Imposter.

I was ordered by a "Criminal Summons" for the appearance on August 2, 2007, in Estancia, County of TORRANCE, STATE of New Mexico; for the pleadings; with a threat of "jail time if I did not show up".

Through my ignorance of what the County and the Court were doing, at the time, I plead "Not Guilty".

As of **August 2, 2007** - the courts ordered "to appoint a Public Defender". (OMG! Here we go again).

Now, I autographed the documents using Upper and lower casing letters of my given name and used the U. C. C. 1 – 207 for the reserve of my rights. However, I was threatened with a $3,000.00 USD fine and/or both a jail sentence of 1,088 days.

The first decision I made was that Mr. Steve Jones or Larry Jones was, in reality "Disqualified" as the judge for this case, because I campaigned against him for the Office of Magistrate and would reflect a conflict of interest. Therefore, he had to "Recuse" himself for conflicting interests. So as of **August 16, 2007**; Steve Jones or Larry Jones "Recused himself".

Now as I understand how the courts in New Mexico work, is if an elected Magistrate cannot adjudicate/try a

7

case, that case is passed on to the higher State Courts and State Judges; which would be a mistake as well. However, I hired an Attorney by the name of Charles E. Knoblauch, for defense. This was a real stupid mistake on my part; but I can claim ignorance and you will understand later within this chapter and other chapters following why it was a "stupid-mistake".

The faxed-documents that were sent to me in **September 17, 2007** was information that I was ordered to supply for Sgt. R. A. Ledbetter who agreed to "dismiss" the case if I were to comply with the following conditions and provide the following information: "i. Warranty deed or Real Estate Contract. ii. State Building Permit. iii. State Solid Waste Permit. iv. Pay $200 application fee. v. Development Plans; and then arrange for an inspector to come out to the property and approve the structure in question".

It continued with the "Removal of all junk materials, C&D materials and trash from the property" and ended with Bring the property taxes up to date." I, as the author and the individual in question, can produce THE evidence to show just how stupid and "ignorant" these Bureaucrats really were and are.

Unfortunately, I did not understand what was in store for me. I did know that under Civil Rights, I had the Right for Privacy"; which includes, "Right to privacy, Papers and Self".

As of **September 17, 2007**, Charles E. Knoblauch and staff "quit" this case, even after paying their required fee; that also included "a letter sent for Complaint to the 'Bar Association' for not completing the contract for representation". Therefore, a "Motion" was sent or the courts for the withdrawal as Counsel"; because counsel was not "representing" the client.

As of **October 12, 2007** - I was sent "Notices to Appear" or be arrested for the "Review of Hearing". The "Notice of Review of Hearing" was changed for November 16, 2007 before Thomas G. Pestak (another elected magistrate in and for another county). I was ordered to appear once again before a Magistrate for a "Review Hearing" on **November 16, 2007** or I would be arrested and jailed.

However, people explained to me at the time, that if there was a "conflict" between a "Magistrate" that the case would have to be presented to the higher courts (State Courts)., It doesn't mean I would win necessarily, it just means that, according to the law and my Civil Rights, I would be heard; or so I thought. (LOL).

On **November 28, 2007** - I was accompanied with two (2) witnesses to the court in Estancia for a "Jury Trial". If I did not show up, once again, I was threatened with being arrested.

I showed up with "witness" which were "locked in a room" and kept away from me and no "Legal Representation" during a "Jury selection" on the same day. This included the same "Threat" that if I did not show up I would arrested and imprisoned.

On the same date, I was arrested for what they charged me with for "Public Drunk". Here is the reality of this charge: 1. there is "no-such-law or charge in the State of New Mexico of "Public Drunk"; 2. I was not drunk; as they claim; 3. I had no witnesses at this conference; and 4. I had no-legal counsel present for any advice guidance or any "Legal Representation". I was transported to "Torrance County Detention Facility"/Correction Corporation of America and processed and held for 7 days within the Segregation Unit, then transferred to Cibola County Jail for the remainder of the "kidnapping". The "Bond" was set for "$10,000.00 Cash only" for my release.

However it did not matter. I was arrested and put in jail for 30 days for a charge that does not exist in law or on the books called "Public Drunk" in the State of New Mexico. After being released I was advised and instructed to leave the state of New Mexico or I would be once again "Killed" for the exposure of what these Evil, Hateful and

Deceitful Bureaucrats with Malicious Intent were doing to other American Victims/Civilians.

So for my self-preservation I left and moved to Minnesota. I again sought a career in Corrections in Appleton, Minnesota within "Prairie Hills Correction Facility"/Correction Corporation of America until they closed that prison down in **2010**.

I realized that if I did not do something to notify "Americans", "U. S. Citizens" or the "Public in General" the Corporate State of California and the Corporate State of New Mexico would "win" and "invent more lies to pad their claims against me". So, I wrote "Your Day in Court: Common Sense"; Published in **2011** through Lulu publishing; the Authors Bradley J. Franks and Robert C. Simpson. This book contains all of the "information" that I saved and added as "evidence" against the Corporate-State of New Mexico and its subsidiary "Torrance County". Our second book, "! AT GUN POINT... Whistleblower's point of view" Published through Author House in **2012**; Authors Bradley – J. Franks and Robert C. Simpson was what took place in the Corporate State of California and its subsidiary "Riverside County".

These books were and are our chance and opportunity to prove to the "General Public" that they are and will be not alone and that there were/are other "Americans" and "U. S. Citizens" that were/are being "abused" by the so-called "Public-Servants".

I went back through all of the information within the books examining the documents, records, and other information I received and was astounded when I came to the realization that the Corporate Government of the U. S. and its Subsidiaries: the Corporate State of California and the sub-subsidiary "Riverside County" and the Corporate State of New Mexico and the sub-subsidiary "Torrance County" had one thing in common... "BREACH OF CONTRACT"!

Remember, the "Government" was and is set up under

three distinct parts: Executive Branch; Legislative Branch and the Judicial Branch". The Executive Branch is for the "Elected" President and his Administration/Cabinet and the "Contract" they have to sign and swear for is/are the "Constitution"; which by the way include the "First Ten Amendments" known as "the Bill of Rights". The Legislative Branch is for those "individuals" who are elected into Office of Senate or Congress and their Office Staff; and well we all understand how the Senate and House of Congress work...lol. However, they too have to sign and swear by the same "Constitution" and "Bill of Rights" that the President and his Administration has to uphold. The final part of the "Government" is the Judicial Branch. This is the branch of Government that tries and hears cases that supposedly makes "sound" Legal decisions that affect all of the people as a whole. The Judges, from the Supreme Court all the way down to the lowest of Traffic Courts and ALL Court Officers are under THE SAME "Contract" that the Executive and Legislative Branch have to uphold. However, the Courts were given a mandate to lie, deny and deceive under "maritime and admiralty courts".

But I digress a little, since this chapter is for the history of our Actions and their Reactions.

On **September 3, 2015** - Robert – C.: [Simpson] and Bradley – J.: [Franks] file a "Lien" against the Corporate-State of California, INC. and the main perpetrators within the action.

On **December 3, 2015** - we sent the "Corporate" government of California presentments consisting of the following: "Lien-Documents; Declaration Letter – Oath Purgatory; Affidavits – Plain Statement of Facts; Our Affidavit; U. C. C. 1; Affidavit; U. C. C. 4; Private Security Agreement; Commercial-Affidavit Statement; True-Bill and Accounting; and Pre-Invoice".

These presentments were received and autographed through acceptance via certified/registered mail. They were given thirty-days (30-days) with a five-day (5-day) grace period for the "response/rebuttal".

The response was Nihil Dicit – Total Silence, Acceptance and Agreement.

On **January 14, 2016** we sent a presentment; a Second-Notice: "Affidavit and Notice of [De]fault and Opportunity-to-Cure" with an allowance of Twenty-days (20-days) with a five-day (5-day) grace period for the "response/rebuttal".

Presentments were received and autographed through acceptance via certified/registered mail.

The response was Nihil Dicit – Total Silence, Acceptance and Agreement.

On **February 10, 2016** we sent a presentment; a Third-Notice: "Affidavit and Notice of [De]fault and Demand-for-Cure" with an allowance of Ten-days (10-days) with a five-day (5-day) grace period for the "response/rebuttal".

Presentments were received and autographed through acceptance via certified/registered mail.

The response was Nihil Dicit – Total Silence, Acceptance and Agreement.

On **February 29, 2016** - we sent a presentment; a Final-Notice: "Affidavit and Notice of [De]fault and Demand-for Cure" with an allowance of Three-days (3-days) with a five-day (5-days) grace period for the "response/rebuttal".

Presentments were received and autographed through acceptance via certified/registered mail.

The response was Nihil Dicit – Total Silence, Acceptance and Agreement.

On **March 18, 2016** the presentment we sent was a: "Notice for violation of Oath of Office 'Breach of Contract' – Demand for Cease and Desist – Notice for Lien – Lis Pendens by Necessity – Subrogation of Autograph/Signature/Authority – Notice for the Suspension of the Charter for the State of California" with an allowance of Thirty-days (30-days) with a Five-day (5-days) grace period for the "response/rebuttal".

Presentments were received and autographed through acceptance via certified/registered mail.

The response was Nihil Dicit – Total Silence, Acceptance and Agreement.

On **April 29, 2016** the presentment that we sent was a Final-Notice: "Affidavit and Notice of [De]fault and Demand-for-Cure" with an allowance of Three-days (3-Days) with a Five-day (5-days) grace period for the "response/rebuttal".

Presentments were received and autographed through acceptance via certified/registered mail.

The response was Nihil Dicit – Total Silence, Acceptance and Agreement.

On **May 20, 2016** - the presentment we sent was a "Notice and Entry of [De]fault by Affidavit" with an allowance of Three-days (3-days); Seventy-two-hours (72 Hours) for the "response/rebuttal".

Presentments were received and autographed through acceptance via certified/registered mail.

The response was Nihil Dicit – Total Silence, Acceptance and Agreement.

"The above-stated presentments met with autograph acceptance through via certified/registered-mail and the time for "response/rebuttal" have/has expired and Res Judicata has occurred against the Lien-Debtors. The [De] fault will be recorded as Public-Record".

"The Lien-Debtors; and All known and unknown Individuals/Agencies/Agents within this action; autograph/ signatures were set by accommodation as per U. C. C. 3 – 415 by the lien-claimants because the lien-debtors are adversaries of the lien claimants, who-caused and injury to-the Lien Claimants' "Birth-Right" of Liberty and Sovereignty. When the Lien-Debtors were confronted-with the claim, they said nothing. NIHIL DICIT"!

"This Lien place-on the Lien-Debtors is not a friendly transaction whereby the Lien-Debtors were willing to-enter into an agreement with lien claimants' quid pro quo, by consent. This lien arose in this manner because no-other remedy for the compensation of the injury is available for the Lien Claimants and the Lien Claimants have/has the right to-use applicable law".

Now I know that this confusing and you are probably asking yourself "Why would these people file a Lien against California and the perpetrators involved in the State of New York"? The answer is simple – New York is the Business-Hub for all the U. S. Corporate Government and the International Community as well.

The "PUBLIC-NOTICE: NOTICE OF LIEN DEFAULT" was placed within the "ROLL CALL" (news-paper) in Washington D. C. The first publication was **August 3, 2016; Vol: 62; No. 8**. The second publication was **September 7, 2016; Vol: 62; No. 10**. The third publication was **September 14, 2016; Vol: 62; No. 14**.

The "FINAL-NOTICE: FORM UCC – Ad" was placed within the "ROLL CALL" (news-paper) in **September 21, 2016; Vol: 62; No.18**.

In **October 21, 2016** - the Lien against California and the Lien-Debtors became a "Lien Surety or Lien Security" through their acts of "Breach of Contract", Negligence and NIHIL DICIT, not to mention the fact that they accepted all presentments through and with their silence.

You are probably asking yourself why we would place the "Public Notice" in the Roll Call (News-paper). This is another no-brainer for the answer...the United States-Corporate-Government is located in Washington D. C. It is the Corporate-Head for all of the 50 States, which are in reality, subsidiaries of the Corporate-Government or equal to the Main Head-Office of a Multi-Billion-Dollar-Corporation.

Now that time has "Legally" expired for a "response/ rebuttal" and the Presentments met with "silence" through "NIHIL DICIT" and the perpetrators remained silent even through the "Legal-Publication" through a very legal "Public-Notice", I had to carry this out one step farther. I asked a Bank if I had to "report" the Interest to the Internal Revenue Service, their reply was "yes, you do"! Accountants and Lawyers also confirmed that I would have to report the Interest as Income to the I. R. S.

As of **October – December of 2016** - as one of the Beneficiaries of the "Lien Security, I "voluntarily-file" a "1040 U. S. Individual Income Tax Return", just for the "Interest" that the "Principle" has been and still is "accruing"; in accordance with the F. D. I. C. "Policy and Procedure" and In accordance with the I. R. S. "Policy and Procedure". Furthermore, 'Policies and Procedures' only apply to those that are employees of that corporation...of which I am not and never will be.

Because the "Principle" is such a large amount, as the beneficiary of a "Lien-Security", it is my choice to "Voluntarily" report the "Income/Interest" quarterly (every three months) not once a year.

I am not an Accountant, Banker, I. R. S. Agent or Lawyer, so if I have made a mistake on filing these documents or used the wrong form – so be it! This is why the word "Service" is part of the Corporate Name in I. R. S.

However, I sent the forms to the Department of the Treasury Internal Revenue Service in Fresno, California. But received a "Response/Threat" from Internal Revenue Service from Ogden, Utah; Dated: February 23, 2017; and "with an Autograph". But their "opinion" consisted of a statement that the "Documents" I sent were "Frivolous Tax Submissions" and they further threatened with an "assessment Penalty of $5,000.00 Dollars". The I. R. S. continues to claim that the "frivolous filing penalty is not included on the notice of deficiency and cannot be contested in the Tax Court".... Who are they kidding?

On **March of 2017** - I re-sent the "corrected forms" per their request and included a second set of 1040 Tax Returns for the Months of **January through March 2017**; with an added statement: "Please do not presume to assume that this is a "Frivolous Tax Submission" by your OPINION. Your Federal Courts, including the Supreme Court of the United States, try FACTS NOT OPINIONS".

The Department of the Treasury Internal Revenue Service in Austin, Texas sent me a "Response/Threat" for what they claim as a "Penalty Assessment" of "15,000.00 Dollars".

Furthermore, the I. R. S. in Austin, Texas sent me an "Amount Due" for Taxes: (please note: I am not going to state what the amount is but I will say that the amount is an eleven-digit amount {$000,000,000.00}).

Now you can realize just how frustrated I became when I read this letter. However, after a couple of days I realized that the I. R. S. (a branch of the Federal Government and a Subsidiary of the Head-Office Washington D. C.) in reality "VALIDATED" our "LIEN SECURITY" against the Corporate State Government of California.

On **August 10, 2017** - I received another I. R. S. Correspondence form Fresno, California. This correspondence was signed as well. However, it turned out to be another "Threat/Response"; "We're working on your account. However, we need an additional 45 days to send you a complete response on what action we are taking on your account. We don't need any further information from you right now". This is the last correspondence. But to set one thing straight...I do not have an "Account with I. R S. It does not belong to me but to them", otherwise they would not be able to do anything without my approval for that "ACCOUNT" or yours for that matter.

Chapter 2

TYPES OF CONTRACTS

There are many types of "Contracts" that Cities/Municipalities, Counties, States and the Federal Government use against its 'Indentured-servants', subordinates or to use the term loosely "people". Some of those "contracts" are as follows: Treaties, THE/The/the Constitution; The/the Declaration of Independence; Intrinsic Fraud; Uniform Commercial Codes; "Oath and Affirmation"; Implied; Pledges; Contract; The/the "Bill of Rights"; "Bill of Attainder/Bill of Pain and Punishment"; or "the 'Strawman theory'" just to name a few.

However, there are many more types of contracts that are posed and created to confound and confuse the American-Civilian People...not to mention, making the contracts one sided, just for the benefit of the contract holder, Politician, Bureaucrat, Lawyer, Judge, Corporate Government with very few exceptions which, in reality, are very few. After all, all one needs to do is read the small/fine print, if you can, as to where you stand within the contract or if you have any 'standing' at all.

One of the types of contract we are going to prove that the Legislative and Judicial part of our government within the United States Corporate Government, Inc. keep breaching with a continued constant [every 2, 4 and

6 years] is called the quid pro quo contract and is also connected with the "OATH OF OFFICE".

The "Oath of Office" or 'Oath/Affirmation' is a quid pro quo contract [as described] in the [U. S. Const. Art. 6, clauses 2 and 3, Davis vs. Lawyers Surety Corporation, 459 S. W. 2nd. 655, 657, Tex. Civ. App.] in which clerks, officials or officers of the government (including Lawyers and Judges) pledge to perform (Support and uphold the United States and state Constitutions) in return for substance (wages, perks, benefits). Proponents are subjected to the penalties and remedies for Breach of Contract, Conspiracy by [Title 18 U.S.C., Sections 241 and 242]. Treason by the Constitution at Article 3, Section 3; and Intrinsic Fraud [Auerbach v. Samuels, 10 Utah 2d 152, 349 P.2d 1112, 1114. Alleghany Corp. v. Kirby, D.C.N.Y., 218 F. Supp. 164, 183 and Keeton Packing Co. v. State, 437 S.W. 20, 28].

There are many types of contracts that the U. S. Corporate Government enforces upon the Americans whether they are legal or NOT and whether the parties honor those contracts or NOT. We will attempt to explain what a contract is, in laymen's-terms, and then explain how the Political-Corporate-Whores are in Breach of those contracts just to line their pockets and Bank accounts at American-Civilian's expense.

The following is the legal definition for the word 'CONTRACT' as defined from Black's Law Dictionary, 6th Edition, page; 322:

Contract. An agreement between two or more persons which creates an obligation to do or not to do a particular thing. As defined in Restatement, Second, Contracts § 3: "A contract is a promise or a set of promises for the breach of which the law gives a remedy, or the performance of which the law in some way recognizes as a duty". A legal relationship consisting of the rights and duties of the contracting parties; a promise or set of promises constituting an agreement between the parties that gives each a legal duty to the other and also the right to seek a remedy for the breach of those duties. Its essentials are competent parties, subject matter, a legal consideration, mutuality of agreement, and mutuality of obligation. Lamoureux v. Burrillville Racing Ass'n, 91 R.I. 94, 161 A.2d 213, 215.

Under U. C. C. (Uniform Commercial Codes), term refers to total legal obligation which results from parties' agreement as affected by the Code. Section 1-201(11). As to sales, "contract" and "agreement" are limited to those relating to present or future sales of goods, and "contract for sale" includes both a present sale of goods and a contract to sell goods at a future time. U.C.C. § 2-106(1).

The writing which contains the agreement of parties, with the terms and conditions, serves as a proof of the obligation.

Contracts may be classified on several different methods, according to the element in them which is brought into prominence. The usual classifications are as follows:

Blanket contract; Certain and Hazardous; Commutative and Independent; Conditional Contract; Consensual and real; Constructive contract; Cost-plus contract; Divisible and indivisible; Entire and severable; Entire contract clause; Exclusive contract; Executed and executory; Express and implied; Gratuitous and onerous; Investment contract; Joint and several; Mutual interest, mixed, etc.; Open end contract; Output contract; Parol contract; Personal contract; Precontract; Principal and accessory contract; Quasi contract; Record, specialty, simple; Requirements contract; Shipment contract; Special contract; Subcontract; Tying contract; Unconscionable contract; Unenforceable contract; Unilateral and bilateral; Usurious contract; Voidable contract; Void contract; Written contract.

There are several other types of contracts and they are as follows: Adhesion contract; Agreement; Aleatory contract; Alteration of contract; Bilateral contract; Bottom hole contract; Breach of contract; Collateral contract;

Compact; Constructive contract; Contingency contract; Entire output contract; Executory contract; Formal contract; Futures contract; Impairing the obligation of contracts, Indemnity; Innominate contracts; Installment contract; Integrated contract; Investment contract; Letter contract; Letter of intent; Literal contract; Marketing contract; Novation; Oral contract; Parol evidence rule; Privity (Privity of contract); Procurement contract; Quasi contract; Requirement contract; Severable contract; Simulated contract; Specialty; and Liberty of contract.

As you can see there are numerous types of contracts that are set out to confuse Americans and they do not fully understand how these contracts work. However, for our purpose we will be discussing the three oldest contracts that apply to all Americans, the Federal Corporate Government and all of its subsidiaries (all fifty (50) States) and two (2) of the three (3) parts of the what makes up the "Government" under the Constitution (and it does not matter which "Constitution") who, by the way, are under contract. Those contracts are: THE/The/the Constitution and The/the Bill of Rights and "Oaths and Affirmations". We will provide facts on how the Political-Corporate-Whores and all of the Judicial Officials/Agents whatever they want to call themselves, are in Breach of these contracts and has been and still is/are covering up this crime against all Americans. Furthermore, we will show you how these 'Political-Corporate-Whores' within 2/3 of the Corporate Government force/trick American Civilians to commit a Federal-Crime just to keep them within the scope of their 'Authority/Jurisdiction' and keep the peoples ignorant of the crimes the Officials and Bureaucrats are committing.

The definition for the types of contracts that we will discuss within this book are taken from Black's Law Dictionary, Sixth Edition, Published by West.

The Declaration of Independence was signed on August 2, 1776. It was/is a founding document that established the structure of our government; States that all men are created equal and each adheres to the same rights and laws; however, there are three parts to the Declaration of Independence; a). The Preamble (it summarizes the principles of our government); b). A list of 'charges' against King George the III of Britain; c). A conclusion (that discusses the call of duty, action and sacrifice).

There are only three 'duties' that an American-National (an individual born on American soil) needs to really focus on and is responsible for; 1). Voting; 2). Jury Duty; and 3). Giving feedback to 'Elected Officials'. However the latter is only if THEY CHOOSE to listen and most they don't.

In truth the Declaration of Independence is a quasi-contract. It is "statement" and a proclamation for Independence that summarizes the principles of our government from a tyrannical-tyrant of Great Britain, with charges that prove the need for independence and a conclusion.

THE/The/the Constitution was signed on September 17, 1787 (according to "Google"). However, some people believe that there are different 'versions' of the 'Constitution' with different wording, punctuation, upper/lower casing letters and sentence-structure that has made a definitive alteration and meaning of what the "REAL" Organic-Constitution embodied. For example, the First Ten Amendments (are articles that create 'minor-changes' within the "Original Document" of the (Organic) Constitution which establishes the basic "Rights of the People": "1. Freedom of Religion, Speech and Press. 2. Right to Bear Arms. 3. The Housing of Soldiers. 4. Protection from Unreasonable Searches and Seizures. 5. Protection of Rights to Life, Liberty, and Property. 6. Rights of Accused Persons in Criminal Cases. 7. Rights in Civil Cases. 8. Excessive Bail, Fines, and Punishments Forbidden. 9. Other Rights Kept by the People. 10. Undelegated Powers Kept by the States and the People".

The reason why we are showing you "THE/The/the" Constitution is to prove that this document is in reality a "CONTRACT" with "We the People of the United States, in Order to form a more perfect Union, establish Justice, insure domestic Tranquility, provide for the common defense, promote the general Welfare, and secure the Blessings of Liberty to ourselves and our Posterity, do ordain and establish this Constitution for the United States of America".

This document is a "contract" between the 'People' and the 'Government' and I mean the "elected officials"; since the "Government" is supposedly the 'People', just like a "Judge" is not the court.

There is one type of 'hidden contract' that any and all parts of the corporate-government that like to use against American-Civilians it is called an "implied contract".

Implied Contract - A legally enforceable agreement that arises from conduct, from assumed intentions, from some relationship among the immediate parties, or from the application of the legal principle of equity.

For example, a contract is implied when a party knowingly accepts a benefit from another party in circumstances where the benefit cannot be considered a gift. Therefore, the party accepting the benefit is under a legal obligation to give fair value for the benefit received. Opposite of express contract. See also express contract, implied in fact contract, and implied in law contract.

In reality an implied contract is a form of 'assumption' and 'presumption'.

Now, this is how 'implied contracts' work: You are under contract from the precise day you are born. The Doctor signs/autographs your Birth-Certificate which has a series of tracking numbers for the Financial Departments of THE/The/the Corporate-Government. Without your knowledge, consent and ignorance these Bureaucrats have just "sold you back into slavery" and have usurped your "Rights" and made you into their "Money-Machine" and only grants you "Privileges" and expects you to pay for them".

The subsidiaries (i.e. City/Municipalities, Towns, Counties, and States) rely heavily on our "ignorance" to keep the Bankers and the U. S. Dollar (conscript) flowing.

In Truth the only difference between the Organized Criminal Practices throughout History of the United States is that they used to call it "Protection-Money". The Corporate Government and its subsidiaries call it "Statutes, Codes and Ordinances" and are done through "License, Permits and Fees". The difference is that the Subsidiaries lay claims or make-up "out and out lies" against those they deem "easy-prey" and take anything and everything they choose too. Not to mention the fact that they destroy lives in the process. Then those that file a "complaint against American–Civilians" use Color of Law just to confuse the real issue.

This is called "constructive-fraud" through their "Legal-Definition". In reality, it is a "BREACH OF CONTRACT" and they can be held accountable for the illegal acts against American Civilians.

To explain "Implied Contracts" a little better for your understanding…if you choose not to believe about your birth certificate; everyone who wants to travel has to "according" to "State Codes" and the individual subsidiaries, has to have a driver's license in order to travel on their highways. Now, all fifty (50) subsidiaries also known as STATES INC. operate under a "Federal Franchise Tax Board" or may be named or called something else like the STATE TAX BOARD; in order to charge you for what they call "their services"? For example, it only costs a STATE INC. approximately $5.00 USD to upwards of maybe $50.00 USD just to print the cards for each individual driver. However, under the "STATE Franchise Tax Board" within the STATE INC. the Department of Motor Vehicles (another subsidiary under the STATE INC. and a DBA (doing business as)) charges $20.00 and more in some STATE INCS. just to apply for the D. L. However, I do digress a little just to show you how the STATE INCS. apply and hook you into an "Implied Contract" and claim that you are "responsible".

So now you have acquired a "contract" that allows you to travel on Highways and roads...but in accepting this "contract" did you pay attention to their offered "contract"? You will notice that on the "license" you have been assigned a number called a "license-number" aka DL NUMBER. It identifies you as the card holder and for the identification purposes for the "STATE INC./STATE FRANCHISE TAX BOARD". Other information on the D. L. is your D. O. B (date of birth) and an expiration date for this "contract". This date is just when the "contract" expires. The next information found on a D. L. is supposedly your name. However, if you examine your "birth record" (another contract) you will notice that your given name is in upper and lower letters this signifies that you are a living-breathing-new-born. But as you grow older and want to travel the STATE INCS. force you into an Implied Contract by making you into a "Corporate Entity" within their "STATE INC. STATE FRANCHISE TAX BOARD" for the sole purpose of collecting USD Funds. This is one of the "hidden contracts" that you are not aware of. Not to change the subject, but other companies under D.B.A. uses your Social Security Number to cross reference your identification, even when it is against the LAW to do so. A lot of arguments have come out of this type contract. Some call it the STRAWMAN theory. Anyway through the "implied contract" and their "Strawman" that they create the STATE INC. enforces all other added "implications" for a "contract" that does not even belong to you. The D. L. may have your likeness and what appears to be your name but it does not belong to you it belongs to the STATE INC. One reason is because if it belonged to you "personally" they could not take it nor suspend it in anyway.

What is even more insidious and ludicrous is that the Internal Revenue Service is operating the same way.

However, they use the TAX Identification number aka the Social Security Number that the CORPORATE GOVERNMENT assigned for your use while you are able to work or you just will not work.

I may be stating the obvious or even making it sound so simplified that the CORPORATE GOVERNMENT, INC. would say I'm "crazy and I don't know what I am talking about". You still cannot hide the truth. Any attempt to expose these practices and you will either be ignored, killed, imprisoned or they will deny it publically and have their puppets clean the mess-up.

The Uniform Commercial Codes are a set of "rules" that the CORPORATE INC. has to follow for corporate business purposes. It defines the parameters of the trade between inter and intra STATE INC. COMMERCE. It further explains how "contracts" are set up, name of the parties that are involved, and the description of all parties' actions of either sale or services. Most, if not all, STATE INCS. have accepted or adopted this form of practice.

What they don't tell you is that you have the right to use those same Codes they do. After all they have made you, an individual, into a "CORPORATE-ENTITY" through the use of their "contracts" whether implied, hidden, written, assumed or presumed.

The next form of contract the CORPORATE GOVERNMENT, INC. and all of its subsidiaries use is an insidious innocuous-appearing (verbal contract) Mantra secretly obligating the victims into accepting representation of their Republic by "THE/The/the United States of America" which fail to properly identify itself or seek open consent and which merely claims to "stand for" the American Republic".

It is the "Pledge of Allegiance" and is repeated in all Public and Private Schools and used for meetings when politicians hold town meetings or even before the city council meetings begin. Note the actual words: "I (which secures a claim of individual consent), pledge (which in reality is an ancient-feudal-act) allegiance (is another form of contract) to the United States of America (which version of THE/The/the United States of America are they referring to?) and to the Republic (this refers to the original organic states' government) for which it stands, one nation under God, indivisible, with liberty and justice for all".

Please understand that there has not been "one-nation" since 1871. There have been two-nations operating under two-separate administrative protocols or guidelines and under two-national-trusts. It has been the subversive objective of Congress to join both "Nations" into one-entity and operate it as an Oligarchy ("which is a form of government wherein the administration of affairs is lodged in the hands of a few persons.")

The "Pledge of Allegiance" is an undisclosed-entrapment into contact ceding authority to represent the individual inhabitants and the American Republic to "THE/The/the United States of America". This is similar to what happens when an unwary individual hires an attorney/lawyer to "represent" them and "stand for" them in a court.

The "representative" gains a largely unaccountable controlling interest in the affairs of their actual employer who is relegated to the status of a ward of the CORPORATE STATE INC., incompetent, or dependent.

The other form of "VERBAL CONTRACT" that is used on a daily basis within the Corporate UNITED STATES, INC. is in the Judicial/Court system. Note the actual words: "Do you solemnly swear (this secures a claim of individual-consent) to (when: past, present or future?) tell the truth, the whole truth, and nothing but the truth, (How can one tell the truth when you don't even know what the truth is?) so help you God?"

As a result of this semantic deceit and duplicity, no-valid-new-contract be-tween the organic American states and THE/The/the United States of America was ever established. In truth, it does not matter which "contract" by the Constitution which the so-called U. S. Corporate Government or its Officers swear to Uphold or Defend they are in "Breach of contract" with all of them.

The above contracts like the Constitution of the United States of America and the Bill of Rights are all written by man and are considered the 'Supreme Law of the Land' written by man for America. However, there is a contract that was written long before the Constitution...that being the "Ten Commandments". In truth the Ten Commandments are actually called a "Covenant" which were written by the finger of "GOD" and set in stone...not parchment, and are still considered the "Supreme Law" over all.

The next chapter is going to consist of Two-actual-cases that the Authors are directly involved with, that will prove once and for all "BREACH OF CONTRACT" and "FRAUD UPON THE COURT" and "CHARGES OF HIGH TREASON" with enough evidence to file against them and remove them from office, bench or authority; not to mention that they lose half, if not all of their pensions.

The following types of contracts are found within Black's Law Dictionary and are presented in alphabetical order. Furthermore, there are many more types of contracts but would defeat our purpose to try and explain each and every one of them. We will insert the definitions for your convenience for those contracts that the UNITED STATES Corporate Government uses.

These are the main kind of contracts that the UNITED-STATES-Corporate-Government use against all Indigenous Americans (Indigenous Peoples that were here before discovery of America), Natural Americans (Americans born on and within the 48 States...excluding Alaska and Hawaii), and U. S. Citizens (People born in another country seeking to become a Citizen of the UNITED-STATES-Corporate-Government).

- **Affirmation** – A solemn and formal declaration or asseveration that an affidavit is true, that the witness will tell the truth, etc.; this being substituted for an oath in certain cases. A solemn religious asseveration in the nature of an oath.

- **Bill of Rights** – A formal and emphatic legislative assertion and declaration of popular rights and liberties usually promulgated upon a change of government; e.g. the famous Bill of Rights of 1688 in English History. Also the summary of the rights and liberties of the people, or of the principles of constitutional law deemed essential and fundamental, contained in many of the American state constitutions. Hamilton v. Hawks, C.C.A. Okla., 58 F.2d 41, 47. First ten Amendments to U.S. Constitution providing for individual rights, freedoms, and protections.

- **Breach** – The breaking or violating of a law, right, obligation, engagement, or duty, either by commission or omission. Exists where one party to contract fails to carry out term, promise, or condition of contract.

- **Breach of Contract** – Failure, without legal excuse, to perform any promise which forms the whole or part of a contract. Prevention or hindrance by party to contract of any occurrence or performance requisite under the contract for the creation or continuance of a right in favor of the party or the discharge of a duty by him. Unequivocal, distinct and absolute refusal to perform agreement.

- **Compacts** – An agreement or contract between persons, nations or states. Commonly applied to working agreements between and among states concerning matters of mutual concern. A contract between parties, which creates obligations and rights capable of being enforced, and contemplated as such between the parties, in their distinct and independent characters. A mutual consent of parties concerned respecting some property of right that is the object of the stipulation, or something that is to be done or forborne.

- **Constitution** – The organic and Fundamental law of a nation or state, which may be written or unwritten, establishing the character and conception of it government, laying the basic principles to which its internal life is to be conformed, organizing the government, and regulating, distributing, and limiting the functions of its different departments, and prescribing the extent and manner of the exercise of sovereign powers. A charter of government deriving its whole authority from the governed. The written instrument agreed upon by the people of the Union (e.g. United States Constitution) or of a particular state, as the absolute rule of action and decision for all departments (i.e. branches) and officers of the government in respect to all points covered by it, which must control until it shall be changed by the authority which established it (i.e. by amendment), and in opposition to which any act or ordinance of any such department or officer is null and void. In a more general sense, any fundamental or important law or edict.

- **Contract** – An agreement between two or more persons which creates an obligation to do or not to do a particular thing. As defined in Restatement, Second, Contracts §3: "A contract is a promise or a set of promises for the breach of which the law gives a remedy, or the performance of which the law in someway recognizes as a duty." A legal relationship consisting of the rights and duties of the contracting parties: a promise or set of promises constituting an agreement between the parties that gives each a legal duty to the other and also the right to seek a remedy for the breach of those duties. Its essentials are competent parties, subject matter, a legal consideration, mutuality of agreement, and mutuality of obligation. Lamoureux v. Burrillville Racing Ass'n, 91 R.I. 94,161 A.2d 213,215. Under the U.C.C., term refers to total legal obligation which results from parties' agreement as affected by the Code. Section 1-201 (11). As to sales, "contract" and "agreement" are limited to those relating to present or future sales of goods, and "contract for sale" includes both a present sale of goods and a con-tract to sell goods at a future time. U.C.C. § 2-106(1). The writing which contains the agreement of parties, with the terms and conditions, and which serves as a proof of the obligation. Contracts may be classified on several different methods, according to the element in them which is brought into prominence.

- **Declaration** – In Common-law pleading, the first of the pleadings on the part of the plaintiff in an action at law, being a formal and methodical specification of the facts and circumstances constituting the cause or action. It commonly comprises several sections of divisions, called "counts", and its formal parts follow each other in this general order: Title, venue, commencement, cause of action, counts, conclusion. The declaration, at common-law, answers to the "libel" in ecclesiastical and admiralty law, the "bill" in equity, the "petition" in civil law, the "complaint" in code and rule pleading, and the "count" in real actions. The term "complaint" is used in the federal courts and in all states that have adopted Rules of Civil Procedure.
- **Declaration of Independence** – A formal declaration or announcement, promulgated July 4, 1776, by the

Congress of the United States of America, in the name and behalf of the people of the colonies, asserting and proclaiming their independence of the British Crown, vindicating their pretentions to political autonomy, and announcing themselves to the world as a free and independent nation.

- **Implied** – This word is used in law in contrast to "express"; i.e., where the intention is regard to the subject-matter is not manifested by explicit and direct words, but is gathered by implication or necessary deduction from the circumstances, the general language, or the conduct of the parties. The term differs from "inferred" to the extent that the hearer or reader "infers" while the writer or speaker "implies".

- **Indemnify** – To restore the victim of a loss, in whole or in part, by payment, repair, or replacement. To save harmless; to secure against loss or damage; to give security for the reimbursement of a person in case of an anticipated loss falling upon him. To make good; to compensate; to make reimbursement to one of a loss already incurred by him. Several states by statute have provided special funds for compensating crime victims.

- **Indemnity** – Reimbursement. An undertaking whereby one agrees to indemnify another upon the occurrence of an anticipated loss. Dawson v. Fidelity & Deposit Co. of Md., D. C. S. D., 189 F. Supp. 854, 865. A contractual or equitable right un-der which the entire loss is shifted from a tortfeasor who is only technically or passively at fault to another who is primarily or actively responsible. Moorehead v. Waelde, La. App., 499 So. 2d 387, 389. The benefit payable under an insurance policy. Immunity from the punishment of past offenses. Lawson v. Halifax-Tonopah Min. Co., 36 Nev. 591, 135 P. 611, 613. The term is also used to denote the compensation given to make a person whole from a loss already sustained; as where the government gives indemnity for private property taken by it for public use.

- **Intrinsic Fraud** – That fraud which occurs within framework of actual conduct of trial and pertains to and affects determination of issue presented therein, and it may be accomplished by perjury, or by use of false or forged instruments, or by concealment or misrepresentations of evidence. Auerbach v. Samuels, 10 Utah 2d 152, 3498 P.2d 1112, 1114. Fraud is "intrinsic fraud" where judgement is founded on fraudulent instruments or perjured evidence or the fraudulent actions pertain to an issue involved in original action and litigated therein. Alleghany Corp. v. Kirby, D.C.N.Y., 218 F. Supp. 164, 183. Species of fraud which renders the document void as, for example, an instrument signed by one who had neither knowledge nor reasonable opportunity to obtain knowledge of its character or its essential terms, is not enforceable even by a holder in due course because such fraud is intrinsic. U. C. C. § 3 – 305(2) (c).

- **Oath** – Any form of attestation by which a person signifies that he is bound in con-science to perform an act faithfully and truthfully, e.g., President's oath on entering office, Article II, Sec. I, U. S. Const. Vaughn v. State, 146 Tex. Cr. R. 586, 177 S. W. 2d 59, 60. An affirmation of truth of a statement, which renders one willfully asserting untrue statements punishable for perjury. An outward pledge by the person taking it that their attestation or promise is made under an immediate sense of responsibility to God. A solemn appeal to the Supreme Being in attestation of the truth of some statement. An external pledge or asseveration, made in verification of statements made, or to be made, coupled with an appeal to a sacred or venerated object, in evidence of the serious and reverent state of mind of the party, or with an invocation to a supreme being to witness the words of the party, and to visit them with punishment if they be false. In its broadest sense, the term is used to include all forms of attestation by which a party signifies that they are bound in conscience to perform the act faithfully and truly. In a more restricted sense, it includes all those forms of attestation or promise which are not accompanied by an imprecation.

- **Pledge** – In common law pleading, those persons who became sureties for the prosecution of the suit. Their names were anciently appended at the foot of the declaration. In time it became purely a formal matter, because the plaintiff was no longer liable to be amerced for a false claim, and the fictitious persons John Doe and Richard Doe became the universal pledges, or they might be omitted altogether; or inserted at any time before judgement; they are now omitted.
- **Treaty** – A compact made between two or more independent nations with a view to the public welfare. Louis Wolf & Co. v. United States, Cust. & Pat. App., 107 F. 2d 819, 827; United States v. Belmont, N. Y., 301 U. S. 324, 57 S. Ct. 758, 761, 81 L. Ed. 1134. An agreement, league, or contract between two or more nations or sovereigns, formally signed by commissioners properly authorized, and solemnly ratified by the several sovereigns or the supreme power of each state. Edye v. Robertson, 112 U. S. 580, 5 S. Ct. 247, 28 L. Ed. 798; Charlton v. Kelly, 229 U. S. 447, 33 S. Ct. 945, 954, 57 L. Ed. 1274, 46 L. R. A., N. S., 397. A treaty is not only a law but also a contract between two nations and must, if possible,

be so construed as to give full force and effect to all its parts. United States v. Reid, C. C. A. Or., 73 F. 2d 153, 155. The term has a far more restricted meaning under U. S. Constitution than under international law. Weinberger v. Rossi, Dist. Col., 456 U. S. 25, 102 S. Ct. 1510, 1514, 71 L. Ed. 2d 715. United States treaties may be made by the President, by and with the advice and consent of the Senate. Art. II, Sec. 2 U. S. Constitution States may not enter into treaties (Art. I, Sec. 10, cl. 1), and, once made, shall be binding on the States as the supreme law of the land (Art. VI, cl. 2).

- **Uniform Commercial Code** – One of the Uniform Laws drafted by the National Conference of Commissioners on Uniform State Laws and the American Law Institute governing commercial transactions (including sales and leasing of goods, transfer of funds, commercial paper, bank deposits, and collection, letters of credit, bulk transfers, warehouse receipts, bills of lading, investment securities, and secured transactions). The U. C. C. has been adopted in whole or substantially by all states.

Please note: there are many more types of contracts that affect and effect all U. S. Citizens and American-Civilians alike and some of them can be disregarded for "Rights" violations and are unenforceable. Furthermore, all parties within a contract must understand what the contract is informing or what each party or parties are responsible for. If either party breaches a contract then that contract becomes void and unenforceable. However, this depends on what the contracts contain within. This includes the contracts from our forefathers who fought to escape the tyranny of the Monarchy of England.

Furthermore, we Americans are under what is known as "Organic Laws of the United States of America". These laws are as follows: (1.) The Declaration of Independence, July 4, 1776; (2.) The Articles of Confederation if November 15, 1777; (3.) Northwest Ordinance of July 13, 1787; and (4.) Constitution of September 17, 1787.

Chapter 3

"BREACH OF CONTRACT"

The idea that a State originated to serve any kind of social purpose is completely unhistorical. It originated in conquest and confiscation, that is to say, in and by criminal actions. It originated for the purpose of maintaining the division of society into an owning and exploiting class and a property-less class, that is, for a criminal purpose! No State known throughout history originated in any other manner, or for any other purpose!

The simple definition of what a contract is as follows: 'An agreement with specific terms between two or more persons or entities in which there is a promise to do something in return for a valuable benefit known as consideration". Unfortunately, the 'Legal' definition is at its basic definition and can involve a lot more variations, circumstances and complexities.

Within this chapter we will point out one specific 'Legal' contract made and entered into by two parties/entities... that contract is called the "Oath" or "Affirmation" or more formally called the "Oath of Office"! As Americans we all know or are aware that after every election all Politicians, Judges, Lawyers, Civil Servants and Bureaucrats are required by Federal Law to sign/autograph an "Oath of office" or "Affirmation" and is to be filed with the Secretary of State for that elected office or filed with the Secretary of State at the Federal level for those Federally elected Officials. However, STATE INCs. (Subsidiaries) may not keep the "Oath of Office" on file but they do have to file them in some sort of "Archives" for future reference.

The contract known as the "Oath" or "Affirmation" or formally known as the "Oath of Office" usually states as follows: "I, (insert name), do solemnly swear that I will support the Constitution of the United States and the Constitution and Laws of the State of (insert name of State); that I will bear true faith and allegiance to the same, and defend them against all enemies, foreign and domestic, and that I will faithfully and impartially discharge the duties of the Office of (insert Title of Office of elected official) according to the best of my ability, so help me God".

The newly elected official or incumbent affixes their signature/autograph on this contract before a Supreme Court Justice, Judge, Magistrate or Secretary of State, after verbally stating the "Oath of Office", dated, then filed with the appropriate office, usually the Secretary of State of the particular State or the Secretary of State at Federal Level for Congressmen, U. S. Senators and the Presidency accordingly. The "Oath of Office" is an example from one of the fifty (50) subsidiaries of the U. S. Corporate-Government. All other "Oaths of Office" may differ in form or language structure. However, they all state that they support the "Constitution" (Federal Document – a contract) and the individual Constitution of the particular State (another contract document); then continues to swear to defend these contracts from enemies, Foreign and Domestic. The "CONSTITUTION" also includes the 'Bill of Rights"...remember they are the first-ten 'Amendments'.

At this point, one needs to understand the "hierarchy" of who's who in the zoo, or rather who's on top, who's on the bottom...or who created whom!

1. The source of all rights came from a Supreme Creator, the Supreme Law Giver.
2. God (the Creator) created man, a Divine-Being, with a soul, flesh and blood and with spirit.
3. Man (We, the people) created and wrote the Constitution, as Thomas Jefferson Said, "to bind them down to the chains of the Constitution" being that they are supposedly 'public-servants'.
4. These so-called governments, State, County, City and national government (Federal U. S., Inc.) were, in actuality, created in artificial corporate capacities. Each State has its own Corporate Seal!
5. These so-called governments were created by and for the people with Christian Principles.
6. State constitutions, with powers and authorities were loosely defined and the Federal Constitution, with powers and authorities were finitely enumerated. (With initial foundation being "The Declaration of Independence" – signed July 4, 1776 – where it was declared that "We hold these truths to be self-evident, that all men are created equal, that they are endowed by their Creator with certain unalienable Rights (sovereignty?), that among these are Life, Liberty and the Pursuit of Happiness...".
7. "That to secure these rights (from our Creator), Governments are instituted among Men, deriving their just powers from the consent of the governed". (Limited Powers!).
8. NOTE: These Rights were 1) Secured and, 2) They are un-a-lien-able. Which means, that your Rights cannot be surrendered or transferred (into privileges) without your consent, example, freedom of speech, of religion, right to keep and bear arms, to marry (without license), right to travel (without 'driver's license'), due process, equal protection of the laws, etc.

9. For the sole purpose of securing Life, Liberty, Pursuit of Happiness and property the people 'elected' men/women as Public/Civil-Servants to serve the people, in their respective capacities in the Legislative, Judicial and Executive branches in these so-called government-corporations.

10. The people did not in any manner, give-up, or surrender or vacate 'their' Rights or their sovereignty, always keeping and holding their 'power' over all of so-called government.

Note that 1 through 5 above create a 'Separation of Powers' Doctrine...on the Private side as against the Corporate Side! We the People, being flesh and blood / 'real' are separate from the artificial-corporate-entities, further supported by following cases for reference:

"But indeed, no private person has a right to complain, by suit in Court, on the ground of a breach of the Constitution. The Constitution, it is true, is a compact (contract), but he is not party to it. The States are party to it..." – Padelford, Fay & Co. vs. The Mayor and Alderman of the City of Savannah, Ga. 438 (1854).

"The people have succeeded to the rights of the King, the former sovereign of this State. They are not, therefore, bound by general words in a statute restrictive of prerogative, without being expressly named. E.g., the Insolvent Law". – the People v. Herkimer, Gentleman, one, &c – 4 Cowen345; 1825 N. Y. Lexis 80.

The Supreme Court in the case of Wills vs. Michigan State Police, 105 L. Ed. 2D 45 (1989)...made it perfectly clear that (I) the Sovereign, [the people] cannot be named as merely a "person" or "any person"!

"All that government does and provides legitimately is in pursuit of its duty to provide protection for private rights, which duty is a debt owed to its creator, WE THE PEOPLE, (Wynhammer v. People, NY 378) ... and the private unenfranchised individual; which debt and duty is never extinguished nor discharged, and is perpetual. No matter what the government/state provides us in manner of convenience and safety, the unenfranchised individual owes nothing to the government". – Hale vs. Henkel, 201 U.S. 43.

"It is not the function of our Government to keep the citizen from falling into error; it is the function of the citizen to keep the government from falling into error". – [U. S. Supreme Court in American Communications Association v. Douds, 339 U. S. 382, 442].

"If the state converts a liberty into a privilege the citizen can engage in the right with impunity". – Shuttlesworth v. Birmingham, 373 U. S. 262.

"The claim and exercise of a Constitutional right cannot be converted into a crime". Miller v. U.S., 230 F 2d 486, 489.

"Officers of the court have no immunity when violating a constitutional right, from liability, for they are deemed to know the law". – Owen v. Independence, 100 S. Ct. 1398.

By Law, if we can prove, and we can, that any Politician, Judge, Lawyer, (or any Political-Corporate-Whore) commits "Breach of Contract" or "Breach of Oath" any Law (I.E.; Statutes, Codes, Ordinances, Misdemeanors, or Federal Laws) are not enforceable against any American.

"Unlawful search and seizure. Your Rights must be interpreted in favor of the Citizen". – Byers v. U.S., 273 U.S. 28.

"This court is to protect against any encroachment of constitutionally secured liberty". – Boyd v. U.S., 116 U.S. 616.

"No state shall convert a liberty into a privilege; license it, and attach a fee to it." – Murdock v. Penn., 318 U.S. 105.

"Where rights secured by the Constitution are involved, there can be no rule (law) making legislation which would abrogate (abolish) them". – Miranda v. Arizona, 384 U.S. 436.

"An unconstitutional act is no law; it imposes no duties; affords not protection; it creates no office; it is illegal contemplation, as inoperative though it had never been passed". – Norton v. Shelby County, 118 U. S. 425.

"The Constitution of these United States is the supreme law of the land. Any law that is repugnant to the constitution is null and void of law". – Marbury v. Madison, 5 U. S. 137.

These cases are actual facts that have been adjudicated by Judges and Court Officers (under "Oath of Office" – a contract) in favor of the American [citizen], not the Political-Corporate-Whores.

With this being said, back to the 'Oath of Office':

The 'Oath of Office' is a "Legal-Lawful-Binding-Contract" entered into with Americans. What can America or an American do if they 'prove' "Breach of Contract" of the '"Oath of Office"? According to the Federal Ethics Committee (there are two – one for the House of Representatives and one for the Senate each has six (6) members); by the way, they too are under an "Oath of Office". A breach of 'Oath' (a contract) is an impeachable offense.

"Impeach"; "To proceed against a Public Officer, a criminal proceeding against a public officer, before a quasi-political court, instituted by a written accusation called "Articles of Impeachment" the formal written allegation of the causes for impeachment, answering the same purpose as an indictment." Black's Law Dict., 6th Ed., Pg. 753.

The Impeachment process does not include added charges that arise out of a "Breach of Office", such as: High-Treason, Organized Crime Activities under the R.I.C.O. Laws (Racketeer Influenced and Corrupt Organizations Laws), Obstruction of Justice, Fraud upon the Court, Fraud from the Bench and Terrorism.

In addition to the above stated charges, Americans can also include: Insider Trading, Money Laundering, Civil Rights Violations and Torts. Here a Tort is; "A legal wrong committed upon the person or property independent of contract (but with a contract in place...it is even better!).

It may be 1) A direct invasion of some legal right of the individual; 2) the infraction of some public duty by which special damage accrues to the individual".

Then there is Constitutional Tort: "Federal statute providing that every per-son who under color of any statute, ordinance, regulation, custom, or usage, of any state or territory, subjects, or causes to be subjected, any citizen of the United States or any other person within the jurisdiction thereof to the deprivation of any rights, privileges, or immunities secured by the Constitution and law, shall be held liable to the party injured in an action at law, suit in equity, *or other proper proceedings for redress. Black's Law Dict., 6th Ed., pg. 1489. Please note the 'italic-under-lined-statement': "or other proper proceedings for redress"; such as a Lien filed against a Subsidiary of the U. S. Corporate Government such as California.

What might be "other proper proceeding for redress"? Why a Private International Administrative Remedy Process... Tort Claim! Where the 'tortfeasor' agrees to and with the monetary damages because he/she stipulates and agrees that he/she violate their 'Oath of Office' in regards to his/her dealings with you, the victim, outside of his/her jurisdiction!

Furthermore, If you, the reader was/were/ or are not aware, it is understood that if a Public/Civil Servant (Political-Corporate-Whore) is Sued three times or, lien[ed] three times (via a tort claim) and possible receives three complaint letters, he/she becomes a liability to the 'insurer', who underwrites their "Performance Bond", their bond is cancelled and the Public/Civil Servant (Political Corporate Whore) is Fired! Along with the importance of the "Oath of Office", if the Public/Civil Servant does not have a 'Performance Bond' on file, they do not and cannot fill the office of that position of their employment.

The following is a simple example of "Breach of Contract" by Public/Civil Servants of their "Oath" for the proof of a pattern for the R.I.C.O. Laws.

You are stopped by police (public/civil servant) for whatever violation. The Police Officer instructs you to produce a License, Registration and Proof of Insurance (which are also contracts).

However, we will use the "Speeding Violation" for our purpose in establishing and exposing a "Breach of Contract" of the "Oath of Office".

The Police Officer, (Public/Civil Servant) for the Corporate Government, uses a device that "measures your vehicle speed" by the use of "radar", a known cancer causing machine. Now, realistically that machine can be "out of calibration" and can give a 'False-reading'. In addition, Police Officers are NOT professionals when it comes to using these machines. However, when the police give you the "ticket" (a.k.a. Bill of Attainder or Bill of Pain and Punishment) the information from the machine is applied as an 'opinion' to the ticket, not fact.

The reason the information applied to the ticket is an "opinion" is because the machine is not perfect and neither is the Public/Civil Servant. Furthermore, it is known as 'second hand information' which is not allowable in a court of law by their "Rule of Law". Courts by law, are supposed to try "Facts" not "Opinion". Remember, Public/Civil Servants, Bureaucrats, Politicians, Judges and Lawyers are under-contract of their own free-will and they cannot claim "ignorance of the Law"...no excuse.

Note: Courts today are not 'Constitutional courts', due to the U. S. Bankruptcy, but are 'Administrative Tribunals'! These tribunals are now involved with Civil Rights Violations in addition to these Political-Corporate-Whores in violation of their "Oath of Office". (See: "The county court is no longer a constitutional court": Fehl v. Jackson County, in re Will of Pittock, 102 OR. 159, 199 P., 2020 P. 216, 17 A.L.R. 218).

You are given the ticket and you have a choice: 1) Pay the fine and accept the inevitable punishments (yes more than one). 2) A court date for the opposition and denouncement of the ticket.

The second choice is where you establish a chain of evidence for "Breach of Contract" or 'Breach of Oath of Office' and all of the perpetrators that are involved. Starting with the Public/Civil Servant known as police.

The 'ticket' (in reality also known as a Bill of Attainder or Bill of Pain and Punishment) is turned into an instrument that will demand that you pay monies for an infraction/ crime you may or may not have committed. As you stand before the Judge (in reality a Foreign Banker), he/she will call your name from the bench and establish you as a 'corporate-entity' under their venue {which turns out to be Maritime/Equity/Admiralty Jurisdiction} (their sphere of control); (meaning-look at the flag behind the Judge...is it red, white and blue? Or does it have a 'gold-fringe around it'?)(This is further evidence that you have been 'forced' into a "Foreign-Tribunal-Corporate-Court"; operated by Political-Corporate-Whores of a 'Foreign-Jurisdiction'). If by chance you try to correct the Judge and the court, by claiming yourself a "living-entity" the Judge and their Court will threaten you with "Contempt of Court". This is, by definition, an act of Terrorism and a "Breach of Contract". Furthermore, the Judge instructs the Court Stenographer (also under "Oath of Office" or Bailiff (Public/Civil Servant: Law Enforcement – also under the same "Oath of Office); "falsify-court-documents" by claiming that you are a "no-show". This is a blatant "Breach of Contract" or "Breach of Oath of Office" with accomplices and witnesses. Furthermore, you can establish "Fraud upon the Court" and "Fraud from the Bench." However, the least common denominator within this procedure is actually "Breach of Contract" and violation of the "Oath of Office", with witnesses. Although keep in mind they will become "hostile witnesses"...They do not like to be caught and will primarily do anything to protect the continuous deception, lie, deniability or whatever excuse just to protect themselves. These self-proclaimed professionals do NOT have license to "victimize anyone in any way shape or form and call it business".

Note: The public/civil servant (Governor, Motor Vehicle Director, Police Officer) have violated their "Oath of Office" in tricking you by misapplication of statutes to obtain a "driver license', as the Motor Vehicle Code only regulates 'commerce upon the highways', hauling people or freight for hire. The State(s) do not make available "Non-commercial Driver Licenses"! So by the police 'Officer' issuing a ticket/citation, he/she are in violation of their "Oath of Office", as you are not subject to the motor vehicle code as your right to travel in your conveyance without a license is a "Constitutional Right", as supported by The Bill of Rights and by Court cases, and the public/civil servant and/or police officer took an oath to uphold and protect the Constitution (a Federal Contract), that your Rights flowing from your Creator to the Constitutions (Federal/State) to state statutes must not be lien[ed], (Unalienable!), in any manner.

From this point forward, we have established a chain of Evidence and Proof (Fact not Opinion) for the "Breach of Contract" (Breach of Oath of Office) and Organized Crime Activities under the R.I.C.O. Laws.

Another important example for the support of the "Breach of Contract" and "Violations of the "Oath of Office" is as follows: "...uphold, protect and defend the Constitution." (This is a Federal Contract) (the SUPREME LAW!). Then why have the Political-Corporate-Whores all violate Article I, Section X of the U.S. Constitution, U.S. Bankruptcy not withstanding? No State shall; ...make any Thing but gold and silver Coin a Tender in Payment of Debts..." However, in truth and Facts those same Political-Corporate-Whores have certainly breached this one and they continue to violate it every day... to your detriment!

In reality the UNITED STATES Corporate-Government

INC. is forcing you as an American-Civilian to commit a "Felonious Crime". Through their Practices and Procedures you are forced to accept their form of payment (U. S. D. Federal-Reserve-Notes) for whatever debts you incur. We all know that "Federal Reserve Notes" are nothing but paper and have no "real" equity involved. But they have to keep you in their "jurisdiction" because of the contract you signed as an infant...remember! Your foot Print! This includes the ignorance of your Birth-Parents...most of them did not know either.

If you were to ask any Political-Corporate-Whore (Politicians, Judges, Lawyers, Bureaucrats or Public/Civil-Servant) if the Laws apply to them, their answer is as follows: "We are not above the Law". If this statement is true made by those corporate personnel in all (50) Fifty States, then as Americans and a "society" it is our Duty to apply those Laws they are not above, and have those Political-Corporate-Whores held accountable for the crimes they have committed...such as Misapplication of Statutes, Fraud, Fraud by Scienter, and many others, because of the very fact they all have violated the very root of their contract... The "Oath of Office".

However, in reality ask yourself this question...What Court, within the (50) Fifty Corporate-States-INC. run by Political-Corporate-Whores is going to adjudicate any crimes brought against anyone of them for "Breach of Oath of Office" or "Breach of Contract"?

The only charge we, as American Civilians, can apply against these Corrupt-Individuals has to start with "Breach of Contract". When that charge is proven (and NOT through their controlled courts) we can apply any other charges that may apply, since they lose 'immunity' from prosecution. This is why these so-called professionals believe they are above the laws.

If any concerned-American writes a letter to their House Representative or Senator about any of these crimes committed against the Politicians or Judicial sector the response usually consists of a "computer-generated response" claiming "We cannot get involved". If you think about this response you will realize that those responses create a connection and a chain of evidence for the continued "Breach of Contract" and "Organized Crime Activities" making them accomplices. Remember, the House of Representatives and the Senators are required "by Law" to take the "Oath or Affirmation" and will support the Constitution of the United States and the State they are seeking to represent. The "Oath or Affirmation" is a Federal Contract not just at State level. So when a Senator or U. S. Representative claims that they can't get involved in a situation because it is not in their "jurisdiction" they automatically become accomplices to the Organized Crime Activities...This is the connection for "Breach of Contract" and sets the pattern for R. I. C. O. Charges.

By Law, if we Americans civilians can prove, and we can, (the Political-Corporate-Whores do not have a monopoly on intelligence); that there is a "Breach of Contract" or "Breach of Oath" any Law (i.e.; Statutes, Codes, Ordinances, Misdemeanors, or Federal Laws) are not enforceable against any American-Civilian. This means, any Individual Political-Corporate-Whore that is in violation of their "Oath of Office" or "Breach of Contract" loses any and all authority within that office or over you or any other American-Civilian.

How can any Judge adjudicate any case when they themselves know that they are in "Breach of Contract" of their "Oath of Office" and sitting on the bench as a criminal? Under these circumstances American-Civilians have an extremely difficult time in winning in any U. S. Court System within any of its (50) Fifty subsidiaries of the U. S. Corporate-Government.

Most Americans, unfortunately, have become complacent and accept the illegal practices committed against them. However, as it stands the courts and Political officers have an abundant list of charges that they can apply against their victims hoping for any, if not all charges, will "stick". As Americans, in our defense, we can only apply one particular charge against them and show irrefutable-evidence of their guilt.

Any and all added charges can be applied when the "Breach of Contract" of the "Oath of Office" has been established. Here, we see a "Tortious (act), defined as; "... tortious is used throughout the Restatement, Second, Torts, to denote the fact that conduct whether of act or omission is of such a character as to subject the actor (the Political-Corporate-Whores both Federal and State and Public/civil servants) to liability, under the principles of the law of torts". Black's Law Dict. 6th Ed., pg. 1489.

What about our/your 'sovereignty, as bestowed by our Creator, and wherein all the American Court (that have ruled on the facts of the matter) has stated in general that "the American people are the sovereign authority"! This means that every 'Oath Taker' from the CEO of U.S., Inc. to Congressmen, Officers of Homeland Security, CIA, FBI, Governors, all State Officers, all County Officers, and all City/Municipal Officers, all of them, by and through their "Oath of Office" are to uphold, defend and protect... our collective and individual sovereignty...within our American form of so-called Corporate Government.

However, they don't recognize our "Rights" through the Bill of Rights or the fact that in truth we, the People, are the "True-Government"; NOT THE POLITICAL-CORPORATE-WHORES. In truth American-civilians have accepted the lie; they have bitten into the poisoned apple of 'progressive-democracy' also known as communism to come against and attack the American-Civilian People and labeling them as "sovereign-citizen-terrorists". This is an oxy-moron if there was ever one. Here again, they all have and are violating their 'Oath of Office' and have and are committing the crimes herein mentioned.

"It's easier to fool people than to convince them that they have been fooled." Mark Twain

The "Police State", as developed here in America, prostituted by elected quasi-government 'Oath Takers', ignorant of the Rights and status of the people, or by design, to subjugate the people away from their rightful position to mere 'subjects' without recognition of "God-given Rights", sovereignty, property rights, all other Rights, enforced and protected in our supposed "Home of the Free and Land of the Brave", makes all of the "Oath Takers", as mentioned within this chapter...all CRIMINALS, IN VIOLATION OF THEIR OATH(S) by "Breach of Contract" and knowingly-guilty of High-Treason, Organized Crime Activities under the R.I.C.O. Laws (Racketeer Influenced and Corrupt Organizations Laws), Obstruction of Justice, followed by other multiple crimes against the Constitution and upon the people they are supposed to serve...Not their bank accounts.

So ask yourself this question, why would you want to interact with them, or do any kind of business with them? All the while, yes, we as American-Civilians, have the right and a duty to hold the Politicians, Judges, Lawyers, Bureaucrats, and Public/Civil Servants (also known in plain English as: Political-Corporate-Whores) accountable for the Contracts that they Breach, but all of them are the 'criminal', they are the true "TERRORISTS"! As the Bible states, "Ye shall know them by their fruit"!

All (50) Fifty subsidiaries of the UNITED STATES Corporate-Government Inc. have applied a program known as P.E.R.S. (Public Employee Retirement System) or something of the equivalent for each individual State-subsidiary by their Charter or State Seal. The Corporate Public Employee is under a Monopoly and is a conflict of Interest against all accused (victims). They receive benefits in fines, fees, taxes, revenue and jail time served.

The Problem with an "Impeachment-Process" is an in-house matter in their "Quasi-Political" Chamber(s), where we can continue to observe them too continue the criminal acts. They, in reality will continue to claim "they are innocent and are just doing their jobs; nothing personal." This is one of the most misleading lies they can ever repeat for their supposed "defense".

But on the alternative, we might also consider that if any (Political-Corporate-Whore) Public/Civil Servant by and through the violation of their "Oath of Office", against any one 'American', wherein such criminal act(s) done is recognized as "High-Treason, Organized Crime Activities under the R.I.C.O. (Racketeer Influenced and Corrupt Organizations Laws), Obstruction of Justice", crime(s) against their Constitution and otherwise to be discovered, then the one so injured can, other than a law-suit or utilizing a 'Tort Claim', can 'NOTICE' that Officer/Department, Office, etc., by certified mail that"...in violation of his/her "Oath of Office", as detailed by the Private Man/Tort Claimant of the deprivation of any rights, privileges, or immunities secured by the Constitution and law and crimes committed, i.e.; High Treason, Organized Crime Activities under the R.I.C.O. Laws (Racketeer Influenced and Corrupt Organizations Laws), and Obstruction of Justice, demands that you and your office, superiors and otherwise cease and desist from further dealings, contact, communication(s) or otherwise with me or to me, otherwise, if you do, each of you, whomever, agree that any such contract or communication with or to me, you agree to pay my fee of $25,000.00 U.S.D. per contact/communication per capita/head/officer, waiver of tort not with-standing and with all Rights Reserved and Preserved".

This chapter gives you the reader something to think about, as your Creator/God-given Rights, as recognized in the Declaration of Independence, Bill of Rights and the United States Constitution, are yours; they ARE valuable! If not accepted, protected, and exercised...then one day soon you may wake-up and find they have been taken from you, though illegally, none the less... taken... and history may have to be repeated in taking them back, if at all possible at that time. So it is imperative to take action now before it gets worse.

Furthermore, the Government, as it stands at this time in our history, is nothing more than a Nom Daguerre (a fictitious "entity"). In truth which government exists? Is it the Government "for the People by the People"? Or is it a Corporate-Government run by "Policy and Procedure" where we American Civilians have no chance of defending ourselves from blatant lies brought or levied against us?

There is a way to go after these self-proclaimed "professionals" by using the same laws they claim they are "not above".

"We the People" can hold their feet to the fire by Filing-Charges of "Breach of Contract" or by placing a 'Lien' against those perpetrators for all injuries incurred. This is the one-charge that is provable, precise, and they will have to answer the charges. However, this type of case cannot be "heard" or "Tried" within the United States Corporate Government as all Judges, Lawyers and Court Bureaucrats are part of the crimes being committed against all American civilians. This type of case can be filed with the International Hague Courts under the heading "Crimes against Humanity", as a 'Class Action Suit' with added charges of acts of "WAR-CRIMES against AMERICAN-CIVILIANS".

As a Corporation, The United States (a corporate government) has and continues to commit heinous crimes through their "judicial-process" against American Civilians. The "judicial officers" claim that they process and Try "Facts" on all cases and that all cases are completely different. This is the first notable "perjury" (LIE) the Officers of the Courts tell their victims. First of all, the "subject-matter may be different" in each individual case, the presentation before their court system is the same...they operate under Admiralty/Equity/Maritime Jurisdiction.

The UNITED STATES INC. Court system, as now operated, is UN-Constitutional. Supreme Court Judges and most Court Judges do not take the constitutionally "required" Oath of Office. These judges commit high crimes and misdemeanors, HIGH-TREASON, R. I. C. O. (Organized Crime Practices), Violation of Sherman Anti-Trust Act (they are a MONOPOLY). Biased, Prejudiced, Union Bar Attorney Judge operates under the law known only to Attorneys and Judges. The Judges and all the court officers that do not swear an "Oath of Office" are not only in "Breach of Contract" but can be brought up on added charges of "Impersonating a Government Official".

The "Court Officers" are already in violation and "Breach of Contract" (un-der the Oath of Office) within their first-case. This is how... 1. NO-full disclosures, 2. Of "Bondage" Contract, 3. Of "Birth Certificate", 4. Of "Social Security", 5. Of "Driver's License". These contracts alone disqualify any and all Judges and Attorneys from representing any case in their "judicial system'. Their attitude is this: "Please, come into our Babylonian Court. We want your Labor, Liberty, Property, and Authority over you. We want more fines, taxes, fees, revenue; or we will put you in jail".

Furthermore, to which "Contract" does the Politicians, Judges, Attorneys or any Bureaucrat take the "Oath of Office" for? We all know that there are at least 2 Constitutions that were written in 1700's 1. Is used for the development of the government "For the People and by the people". The other was to keep American-Civilians ignorant and confused just so they can "screw-everybody-over" within their 'authority or jurisdiction' to help fatten their bank accounts or defend the "King's-Money".

We are going to start off with the one-contract that everyone seems to be in agreement with...the "CONSTITUTION"...it is a "CONTRACT" – a majority of the Politicians, Judges and Attorneys agree that "the Constitution is a contract"...more-over we will point out the "Oath/Affirmation" of Office before any politician can assume the Office he/she was elected for. This includes Judges, Attorneys, Police, basically any and all Public-Officials – City, County, State and Federal Incs.

A contract is a two-way street...just like trust. We trust those we elect into office to do the right thing and not concentrate on their personal pocket books or Re-election funds or false-persecution, prosecution, false-statements in general, or false-swearing etc., etc.... by BREACH OF CONTRACT.

The "CONSTITUTION" and the ten (10) Amendments: (the Amendments also known as the Bill of Rights are part of the "Constitution")... a "CONTRACT".

But, everyone is looking for the so-called "silver-bullet" or "sword" to put a stop to the Criminal actions against American Civilians from those that "claim" superior knowledge...because of a higher education?... "Polly-Parrot" strikes again. This is why "LADY-JUSTICE" is blind-folded...and yet carries a scale to weigh the FACTS and TRUTH against "untruth". I will explain the "POLLY-PARROT" statement further along in this article.

However, let's start with the definition of the word "Contract". The definition is extensive and can be found in "Black's Law Dictionary".

The Definition of the words "Contract Law" is as follows: "The body of law that governs oral and written agreements associated with exchange of goods and services, money, and properties. It includes topics such as the nature of contractual obligations, limitation of actions, freedom of contract, privity of contract, termination of contract, and covers also agency relationships, commercial paper, and contracts of employment".

The "Oath of Office" or Affirmation of Office is one that is an Oral and Written Contract for Americans. The Oath of

53

Office is as follows: "I, (Official states name here), having been elected to the office of (insert office-title), (District, Division and State), do solemnly swear that I will defend the Constitution of the United States and the Constitution and Laws of the State of (insert name of State), and that I will faithfully and impartially discharge the duties of said office to the best of my ability".

The "Oath of Office" is subscribed, sworn and autographed before a District Judge, Secretary of State, or State Attorney General who act as witness for this contract then they too autograph the "Oath of Office/Affirmation as a 'Witness'.

Remember, these 'people' are supposedly "Highly-Educated" and graduates of prestigious Colleges or Universities. This is why I call them "Polly-Parrots" because they are not learning something new under Law or Political Sciences (which is just a joke)... they are just repeating the same old information and not adding any new thoughts or approaches for any of the problems facing American-Civilians or U. S. Citizens. In other words they keep compounding the same mistakes over and over...not unlike the Medical field, Physics, Astral Physics or even Computer Science where those fields are making new discoveries and actually finding something new on a daily basis whether it is good, bad or indifferent.

However, back to our discussion about "Breach of Contract" otherwise known as the "golden-key".

Let's say you as the reader of this article are under many contracts...and you are! The first contract your parents autograph is your "Birth-Certificate". However, you also as a first-born-infant sign as well... your "foot-print" with a number attached to be used by the Corporate Government to be levied in and used through their Banking system.

The next contract you and your parents Autograph is the "Social Security" which in reality is a "Corporate" number that identifies you 'personally' used for employment purposes, yet another number. In this example, you have been attached to a 9-digit number for the Social Security for work "Privileges".

The next contract you autograph for is the "Driver's License or Identification card". The driver' license is, if you noticed, all in capital letters making you into a mini-corporation known as a Nom Daguerre (a fiction); with yet another set of numbers. My point in using the above contracts is this...if we, as American-Civilians, have to abide by or conform with or even accept this type of business practice (these contracts are established by the Uniform Commercial Codes...and are another form of contract including, oral, written or implied etc. etc.) then so does the Senate, Judicial and Executive branch and employees of the Government. But if you have noticed the Government Officials have considered themselves above the law through their actions and claim they can do anything they want legally or not.

However, the "magic-key happens to be "BREACH OF CONTRACT". This applies to ALL bureaucrats and their so-called security-departments including all of the police force across our nation.

Let's use "FRAUD UPON THE COURT" as a prime example...because most American-Civilians do not seem to understand how the courts work or how a Judge adjudicates or come to the decisions they do on any case in front of them. In addition, most of the cases that are adjudicated by the court officer or judge is by "opinion" not fact. By the way, all court officers...from the judges, lawyers, stenographer, and bailiffs/sheriffs are under "contract". They are under a "sworn oath of office"...once again by the "Constitution". Now there seems to be some misunderstanding about the Constitution...It does not apply to individual Americans...but it does set limitations to what the Corporate Government, Inc. can do to Americans. With that said, the one contract that was added to the

Constitution is called the first Ten Amendments as we know them as our Civil Rights and is commonly referred to as "The Bill of Rights". NOT A BILL OF PRIVILEDGES!

If the Courts or any of its officers or any Politician under a sworn oath or Affirmation of Office violate your "Rights" that particular Court District, City, County, State or Federal Agency loses all jurisdiction, control and authority of the case under "Breach of Contract". Remember, the Oath of Office is a contract.

I contacted the State of South Dakota, State Attorney General, Marty Jackley and his staff and asked his department a simple generic question..."Are any contracts (such as: Verbal, Implied, written, treaties, compacts, etc. etc.) enforceable if either party Breaches the contract or covenant"? The second part that question is as follows: Would this apply for-living "persons" as well as Business and Corporations alike"?

First let me say that I am withholding the name of the individual from the State Attorney General's Office (which was an attorney) that gave this ludicrous insidious answer... "The question you asked is a legal question. You will have to ask an attorney"...lol! To my surprise I thought I was speaking to an Attorney, I mean he claimed to be an Attorney with the State Attorney General's Office.

However, this is my interpretation, my answer or opinion, as far as my understanding about 'Breach of Contract"... All contracts become "null and void" and unenforceable if either party Breaches it, by LAW! This means you cannot be punished for a crime or breach if you can prove that any Agency-Officer/Government-Agent is in breach. We may not win monetary-compensation through their controlled courts...but we will win the point of argument or contention. In easy terms, the corporate government loses what little "authority" and "jurisdiction" they think they have over us. This is why the Court Officers use "Threats, Duress, and Coercion, Collusion and Subterfuge" against their victims.

For example, your car insurance, life insurance, or any type of insurance or contract you autograph will become "null and void" if you stop paying the premiums, Right? The same thing works for the Politicians and all Government Officials...but they do not want you to know this...after all they believe they are doing a "good job"... which amounts to being just Bull-Shit!

The court system itself is geared to separate you from your hard earned money that does not belong to you and split it between the court officers...the judge being the chief officer; and in some cases the judge is acting as a banker representing those who are "embezzling and extorting" monies from innocent individual victims.

The key with "Fraud upon the Court" is the simplicity of the matter when you have identified that the opposing party has "purchased-injustice" by buying out the officers of the court. The "Attorney of Record"...the one you pay exorbitant fees for to represent you..."works in concert" and is instrumental in the "Law and Motion Waltz" ultimately withholding critical "Material Evidence" from being admitted on your behalf.

"Please note: Fraud Upon the Court is fraud which is directed at the judicial machinery itself. It is not fraud between parties or documents, false statements or perjury".

Fraud upon the Court is commonly associated with "Extrinsic Fraud". It deals directly in withholding information by "Omissions". It is a specific form of fraud that allows the "Attorney of Record" (your attorney) to use "Attorney Client Privilege", "Excusable Negligence", "Plausible Deniability", and "Omission" for critical facts that would allow the aggrieved party no-means the establishment for a "Cause of Action". Furthermore, extrinsic fraud is typically accompanied by "Demurrers, Motion for Summary Judgement" and other means of avoiding "Discovery" that regards the "Gravamen of the Complaint". The result for the solution for the aggrieved party is usually a "Declaratory

Judgement" without relief which is a proven means in accordance with the "Evidence Code".

The courts like to use this excuse when you lose..."Sorry! No Hard Feelings...but Business is Business". When a person enters the court and/or the court system they go through a wide-range of emotions. You have to remember, although it is difficult at the time, to keep your emotions in check... because the matter is not an emotional one...just strictly "business". You have to remove the emotional-ties and emotional-entanglements. You have to strictly adhere with the "Law and Motion Waltz" (which is nothing but a dog and pony show at a three-ring circus). However, we now know that we can turn-the-tables back on them so-to-speak. These self-proclaimed professionals within the court system will use any tactic and/or distraction to play on your emotions for the distraction away from the shear simplicity of a "Declaratory Judgement" in your behalf. Keeping your Gravamen of the Complaint in simplicity and related with the Controversy in question will help you establish a Cause of Action.

A Law and Motion Waltz, is a dog and pony show that is usually headed up by YOUR "Attorney of Record" (which in truth does not exist) for your benefit to make you think and believe he/she is doing a great job and is on your side. Here is the simple truth within this matter...when the courts suspect that you believe that they are fraudulent, the courts will set a "Trial" date and do what is called a "Law and Motion Dump". In reality, your attorney of record, whether he/she is the lead person or just following the judge's-instructions is working in concert, with the court and is putting a on a circus-show for "POMP and CIRCUMSTANCE". The Prosecution and/or the Defense Attorney would do the same under Pomp and Circumstance.

Your Attorney of Record was given the ability to act and speak on your behalf (by you!...A Contract! You autographed it.) Furthermore, you do not have a direct-voice within their court. This is the means that allows blood-money to be dissipated through the court wherein the officers of the court end up with a majority if not all of the blood-money and the party that committed the initial-fraud gets off by allowing the officers of the court to take what they want from the blood-money. Remember all Officers of the Court are working in concert. This means ANY attorney you hire will most likely and certainly participate in Fraud upon the Court or the other officers of the court will ultimately report them to the State Bar for some sort of reason. Furthermore, and this is usually what happens, if the judge is "on the take" your attorney will ultimately side with the court and take a bribe as well. This is called..."Legal-Malpractice". This terminology is known as a misnomer and an OXY-MORON. The definition of "Legal" and "Malpractice" is defined within Black's law Dictionary. However, the terminology cannot be found-together for the definition. There is no such word within Black's law dictionary as "Legal-Malpractice". Both of these words are opposites (and no they do not attract). There is actually no-such word found in Black's Law Dictionary... individually yes...but not as a two words placed together or as a compound-noun. The word "Legal-Malpractice" does not exist. If this is the case then Doctors, Physicians, Surgeons or even Nurses cannot be held responsible for their "Malpractice". The reason is because you "hold them blameless" for any mistake they make. However, through example we know that his is not entirely the truth.

In any event, if your attorney is not engaged against you then the reality of the situation is that the opposing counsel or attorney is engaged in "Malicious Prosecution". This is an attorney that uses their authority over a litigant directly engaged in actions that are directly targeted to hold the litigant in actions that would be the same as "Vexatious Litigation". One of the ways the attorneys like to cover-up their fraud is to commit more fraud in the hopes that they will place you in default. One reason is because the cycle becomes more pronounced and they fear that their "Bar-Card" (not a license) is at stake...This also includes the Judges "Bar-Card". However, be aware these so-called professionals will resort to "Entrapment" too cause more damages against you and your "case".

Furthermore, to inform you of how crooked this particular part of the government is...this is what they do to confuse you even more...they "Fabricate-Evidence" for the benefit on their illegal-actions over a long period of time with extensive litigations to hide any and all "Omissions." The court system is set up to deny the 'Facts' in the case that are clearly within your possession, withholding critical information through Omission and ultimately unleashing fraudulent and fabricated evidence during the trial; and the judge will simply admit this at the trial.

The "Omission of Evidence" during a trial is a fraud, not to mention the fact it is against the "Evidence Codes". As they conduct this fraud, they are careful not to present direct evidence that is fraudulent based on wanton Omission. However, they do not fabricate the evidence until the "Trial". Wherein the Material Misrepresentations and Inconsistent Declarations are made to focus on the efforts away from the wanton omissions. Now by their laws the "Statute of Frauds" and "Errors and Omissions" come into play.

But here is the explanation of "Plausible Deniability". The fact is when lawyers are engaged in "Fraud Upon the Court" they are looking for a means of creating a "hook" that will cause your case to ultimately lose by omission of critical evidence. In this manner, your attorney has Plausible Deniability that the omission ever existed. Unfortunately, you have to prove that your attorney actually took direct "Acts" to hide the omissions from being produced or introduced into evidence. (However, by "Breach of Contract" we can.). By the time you figure out that you have been "Screwed" over by your own attorney, he/she is long gone from the case, the judge has dismissed him/her from the case because you stopped "paying" them, ran out of "money" or unable to continue to pay them. In self-defense, your attorney can and will directly state that there is a lack of evidence for the proof that they have omitted any facts intentionally. Furthermore, the opposing attorney and judge will cite that the issue was never raised by opposing counsel and therefore your attorney did not have any need to bring the matter into evidence or into the case. Therefore, Plausible Deniability is the key to finding this Omission and all the circumstances that relate to it.

Both Attorneys and the Officers of the court that are against their clients ultimately leave the clients without any admissible evidence, the matter is set for "Pre-Trial" where no further evidence is admissible and the client's own counsel admits to the court that they "informally" accept the evidence on behalf of their client. However, the client will no longer be able to communicate with his/her counsel about any of the evidence he/she accepted. The client is set for "TRIAL" with no means of admitting evidence for the pending trial and his/her own counsel has ultimately requested to be removed from the case. By these actions, there is no-chance of even having a "fair-trial" and the matter is not merely being able to admit evidence or object to any of the "Fraudulent-Evidence" that the opposing counsel will unleash on the court at the "Trial". The judge ultimately accepts any and all fraudulent evidence by the favored party and denies the defense against fraudulent "Allegations". Leaving the result that the judge does not need to "rule" on the merits of the case but rather on the "Admission and Objection" for the "Facts in Evidence", that will be used as the deciding factor of the case.

These are the "Basic Principles" that involve "Facts in Evidence, Conclusive Presumption, Material Misrepresentation and Plausible Deniability". There is a loophole: the loop-hole that directly causes most all Fraud upon the Court Cases to look alike is based on the attorney that relies on the basic principles of "Attorney Client Privilege, Excusable Neglect, and Plausible Deniability".

Within the Evidence Codes there is a presumption of what a "Reasonable Person" would infer from "Circumstantial Evidence". (Your attorney failed to explain any of this to you). In reviewing your case, it becomes obvious that all of the court officers "Work in Concert" to create a cloud of litigation that allows their opinion for "Plausible Deniability".

Furthermore, to make matters even worse and confusing the Court Officers "Mirror your claims to confuse the issue". When you state a claim it will most likely be turned into a claim against you in order to confuse the issue. Unfortunately this is a very common practice in Fraud upon the Court case. By them making outrageous claims against you it confuses the issue and it allows them to diffuse your claims you made against them. If you claim "Money Laundering" and "Embezzlement", they will make the same claims against you but with a twist...they will pile more outrageous charges against you, even if they do not have any evidence to back it up. Eventually you will have a claim for "Defamation of Character", Liable and Slander in a following-case because their claims are clearly unfounded and filed with malicious intent.

What most American Civilians or U. S. Citizens do not seem to understand is where is all the money coming from? Well, here it is in a nut-shell, it's called "Blood-Money" that fuels this particular type of Fraud upon the Court. It requires the opposing litigants who actually commit the Initial Fraud, Deceit, Material Misrepresentation, Inconsistent Declarations, Money Laundering, I. R. S. Fraud, Embezzlement, etc. etc. etc. against you has "Blood-Money" and that they cannot keep it unless the attorneys and the court are complicit (in total agreement) and working in concert to conceal the "Omissions", "Inconsistent Declarations and Material

Misrepresentations". These will ultimately result in providing a "Plausible" story that will only be revealed within the "Trial".

The reality of hiring your own counsel will prove for "Fraudulent Evidence". Your own counsel will be directly involved in making sure that none of the evidence "you provide and are in possession of" that would prove your innocence is never provided for the court. Furthermore, your own counsel will informally advise the court that he/she accepted evidenced from the Opposing Counsel... however, that evidence will never be provided for you and that the so-called evidence against you cannot be contested. The Judge only needs to inform you that you should not have dismissed your counsel and that your prior counsel accepted the evidence on your behalf; even if your counsel quit or asked to be removed from your case.

The idea of the court system, the judges and the court officers, as it stands, is to have all of them working against you. This is called "Working in Concert". Any attempt for you to claim "conspiracy" is directly dismissed by the court. Any attempt for you to "admit-evidence" is directly dismissed by the court. Any attempt for you to expose the "Fraudulent-Evidence" that was presented as a (subterfuge tactic) as an ambush during the "trial" is directly accepted by the court without any qualification. By the "Judicial-Reality", the matter is set-up by the court and all of the officers within that court, to directly rule against you after the "trial" without objection. During the trial the court does not need to evaluate any "Cause of Action" against them since the "Fraudulent-Evidence" was accepted against you without objection. "How can you defend yourself against "Perjury" without evidence"? The judge does not need to rule on the case, all the court did was admit and deny "Material-Evidence".

The court officers working in concert create a "cloud of litigation" in order to hide the Fraud upon the Court. This is known as "Creating a Cloud of Litigation". They attempt to hide the fact that most, if not all, of what is happening is an attempt to hide a "Wanton Omission". They do this to create the "impression" that justice is being served within this "extensive-litigation" that is intended to give you the impression that your attorney is actually doing something to further your cause or case. "Believe it or not"! This is the farthest from the truth or facts.

In truth "your own counsel is harming your case". During this "Cloud of Litigation" your counsel is "instructed" either by the Judge or by the "Opposing Counsel" too "skew" the evidence, which proves your innocence, by hiding your evidence and not objecting to the fraudulent material misrepresentation brought against you. Your attorney will put on a show of "Pomp and Circumstance" much like a circus-parade before the main-event or show. What your attorney is doing at this time against you is called "sandbagging". Your counsel is merely following the instructions of opposing counsel and the court in compliance with any and all requests through "Law and Motion". In reality both counsel, are merely giving the impression that they are working hard and charging massive fees for the compliance with any and all requests that the court and opposing counsel are demanding. Your counsel will explain or inform you that your "account" is daunting and the requests are massive. Your counsel will further explain and inform you, that the ""Cloud of Litigation" will cause lots of problems for them and take up most of their time in the attempt for your defense". Your Counsel will then inform you that they need to be relieved as your counsel, unless you produce as much "payment" as possible and "bill your account" without creating a suspicion that they are merely depleting your resources prior to setting you up for the "Pretrial Dump". In truth, through their actions, your counsel is merely depleting your resource, making sure that none of your evidence is properly admitted for the court and also allows the opposing counsel to admit evidence that is completely fabricated. The reality of this is that both-counsels, (your counsel and the opposing counsel) are committing "Legal-Malpractice" and the court is complacent and complicit with the allowance of the parties to do so.

The "Blood-Money" that rightfully and ultimately belonging to you is being used against you and all of the "Officers of the Court" directly benefit at your expense. Your own counsel is doing most of the harm for your case as your attorney of record. They do the most harm since anything they do – on your behalf – will ultimately result in that action being recorded by the court as "your direct statement".

We have discussed both counsels (your counsel and the opposing counsel) but have not addressed the "Ring-Leader of the Circus"...the Judge. I understand that in life there is no-such thing as "absolutes". However, it is "absolutely" ridiculous to believe that the Judge (which is the ring-leader of this circus) is not on the take or even leading the "feeding-frenzy". Any "Reasonable-Person" that sees or even notices, just a glimpse of the depravity or subterfuge and sheer wicked behavior that results from this complete and utter debauchery of the "legal-system" would surly know that, by definition, this is "Fraud". The Judge has to sit through-a-complete two-years of this "Cloud of Litigation" that your counsel and the opposing counsel have created. The Judge has to maintain a great deal of avoidance in order to maintain "Plausible Deniability". The judge has to maintain as much distance from the matter or "subject-matter" as possible as the "feeding-frenzy" attacks the "struggling-swimmer". Keep in mind that both counsels (yours and the opposing) will gladly throw themselves at the "mercy" of the courts...lol! (What mercy?), in order to protect the judge. In turn the Judge will protect the attorneys if the matter is brought before the court or before the "State-Bar". When the Judge is involved in "Fraud upon the Court" they will focus the efforts on your counsel to lead the direction of the fraud. Many cases that involve "Fraud upon the Court" will have many counsel or attorneys that will represent your interests. They will come at you one after the other, those that take the case, but will intentionally cause more damage than they ANSWER. Because of this, the "Declaratory Judgement" without relief will allow your case to move forward for the resolution of the "Basic-Issue". If you attempt to find an "HONEST" counsel or attorney it will NOT prove fruitful. If you decide to be the "Pro-se-Litigant" the Judge will dismiss any and all pleadings you have strictly on the basis that you are not represented by "counsel of record" (which in truth does not exist). In addition, you as the moving-party do-not have a voice in their court. In this way the Judge is trying to "FORCE-YOU" to hire an attorney or counsel that they can coerce, threaten or use subterfuge into engage in their fraud.

Most of the cases that deal with "Fraud upon the Court" take advantage of the "lower-income" bracket of American-Civilians. It's like a school of sharks hunting for injured fish for an "easy-target". If you prove that you are NOT an easy target they will leave you alone. However, remember they have been in this practice for some-time and this is not their first-feeding-frenzy. The reality is this, more than likely there is a "Class-Action" Lawsuit, in the works, if you are successful and it is not just you that would be suing them if this was exposed. It would be in their best interest to negotiate and NOT be exposed. If you know of any other victims that have been targets in their past endeavors it will help in providing substance and weight for your "Cause of Action" against the "feeding-frenzy"...they are out there and you will find them. There are many cases where the "Feeding-frenzy" was exposed and the matter turns into a "Class-Action-Suit".

The goal of your counsel and the opposing counsel is to deplete your funds and resources before a trial. This is how the court-system-works by their ultimate-goal, (1). Your counsel stacks your evidence against you, (2). They deplete your funds, (3). They set your case for "Pre-Trial", (4). Then "Withdraw" as your counsel of record, (5). Then leave you penniless and Defenseless and Devoid of "Material-Evidence" before the "TRIAL" is set. Now here is the stinger, your counsel will, with most certainty, be generously compensated by the opposing counsel and the Judge for devastating your case at which time your counsel will "defame" you before the court and tell the court that you owe them a "balance that is unpaid". The Judge (the banker) and the court will, undoubtedly, view you and your case with "Contempt" before the trial is set. Every-one of your counsels, (that you have hired and involved within your-case) have completely devastated your case and is directly compensated from "Blood-Money"...the funds that were stolen from you by the "Opposition".

The "Law and Motion Dump" defines a specific-procedure that results during the "Law and motion Waltz" when you discover that your counsel is leading the "Fraud upon the Court" against you. Your "counsel of record" knows full-well that they are liable for "Legal-Malpractice" if you should discover that they are acting against your interests. At this point, the "feeding-frenzy" is simply waiting for the matter to go before the "Pretrial". This allows your counsel to petition the court and withdraw on the basis that you are not willing to pay "exorbitant" fees for the continuation of their representation of the misrepresentation for your case for the "TRIAL" that they set-up. If your counsel is not willing to help you during the case why would they be any better during a trial?

With so much information being brought against you and your case, "finding a resolution" may not be simple. In reality, you have to understand how to identify and understand the "Gravamen of the Complaint", "Establish a Cause of Action" and prepare a "Declaratory-Judgement".

An "Appeal" is not appropriate since the case is not riddled with technical-errors but rather with

"Intentional-Fraud". In "Fraud upon the Court" the matter is much more related to "Extrinsic-Fraud" and your petition would directly bring the action back in on the findings for the "material-facts". The "Statute of Frauds" defines that in the event of "fraud" the Statute of Limitations, "Collateral Estoppel" and "Res Judicata" do-not apply. The subject-matter or the "MATTER" can be re-dressed and/or addressed within a "new-petition" well after the normal "Statutes of Limitations" are long expired. The finding of the "Omissions" that were adamantly and intentionally withheld due for fraud becomes the way to bring back the "Subject-matter" or "Matter" back in on a new petition.

If you are an "injured-fish" you would never be able to define an "Architectural-Blueprint" that could and would resolve your case. The "architectural-blueprint" in your case is called the "Factual and Procedural History" and the "Memorandum and Points of Authorities". However trying to find an "honest" counsel that will help in the exposure of a Judge, Prominent Businessmen and their Corrupt Counsels will be futile. After all, there are Judges and Counsels that have been arrested, disbarred and held in prison for NOT playing the game (lose term) that a majority of the courts are playing. I agree - none of this is a game. However, they need to be stopped and exposed once and for all.

If you choose to take the chance to represent your-self within a case through their courts, you need to at-least find a counselor that will agree with a "Limited-Scope of Representation" with a viable option for a "Declaratory-Judgement". If your counselor is willing to guide you as a "Pro se Litigant" They will help you create your "architectural plan" by "Establishing Your Cause of Action" for the exposure of the "Omission" through a "Declaratory Judgement" or through a "Motion for Summary of Judgement"; that is related directly with the "Gravamen of the Complaint". If you come before a judge that is "corrupt", your counsel – no matter how honest – you may think they are will have no-choice but to "Throw you under a bus" in other words "sandbag" you. If you have a truly-honest-counsel they will not take the case directly as an "Attorney of Record" and will help guide your case through solving the "Gravamen". It would literally be "political-suicide" for a counselor or an attorney that has a State-Bar (not a license) too take on a litigant, if you are able to gain a "Declaratory-Judgement" that regards your "Gravamen", you will have re-solved approximately 80% of your case. At this time the "honest-Attorney" will be safe to take the "SIMPLE" part of the case. They will look at your "Factual and Procedural History" and help in making improvements. However, if the so-called "Honest-Attorney" merely looks at the "Factual and Procedural History" and tells you that it will not work, never explains to you why, and/or does not provide an alternate route, then beware. All that the counselor wants to do is to play the "Law and Motion Waltz" and throw you under the bus or once again "Sandbag you" and your case.

As you approach this problem, based on the aforementioned circumstances, you find yourself in a situation similar to the one "David" found himself in when he faced an expert-warrior "Goliath" with an undefeated mighty army behind him. However, the "Omission" and the "Gravamen of the Complaint" becomes your "Stone" that ultimately defeated Goliath. You need a "Declaratory Judgement" on your very issue and you will be home-free and your case becomes 80% resolved. However, you may have to resolve the gravamen on your own because you will be unable to find an Honest Counsel that will take on the case. Beware of those that claim that they are "Honest Counsels" and merely does the "Law and Motion Waltz". If you act as your own counsel known as a "Pro Se Litigant" (Oh! By the way...most judges will scoff and add their personal slur against you because you, in reality, know more about your case (Gravamen) than a counsel does) and you understand the art of "Negotiation", you can most likely resolve the "Gravamen". You will have to maintain an offensive strategy through a barrage of litigation thrown against you by multiple sources attempting to create a cloud of litigation that ultimately is intended to discourage you and distract the court from the Omission and the gravamen that you are attempting to resolve. Furthermore, if there is a possibility of a class action lawsuit, it may be prudent to couple up with another "victim" that was the prior subject or current subject for the courts feeding frenzy. Remember this is not the first time for a feeding frenzy. Once the "sharks get a taste for blood they seem to be compelled to repeat the process" whenever another struggling swimmer comes within their sights/cites. You have to be able to prove that you have the direct ability for the litigation for the gravamen and the "Sharks" will take you seriously.

The last step within this part of the article consists of a "Declaratory Judgement". In truth your case is a "blind intersection" because you cannot see the solution due to the "Errors and Omissions" created by your counsel. However, a "Limited Scope of Representation" is a possible solution for moving forward. The only way for you to recover from "Fraud upon the Court", if you are the "Pro Se Litigant" is to get a "Declaratory Judgement" that relate with your "Gravamen of the Complaint". In many cases you can bring "Facts in Evidence" from your discovery through "Errors and Omissions".

This article appears in the 'American's Bulletin' Volume 44 Issue 09/10 to show just how "Unprofessional", "Opportunistic", and "Nasty" the Court and their Officers are in reality. However there is one other way to get this part of the government off your-back. Remember, every Judge, Attorney (counsel), Bailiff/Sheriff, Stenographer...ALL Court Officers are supposed to have an "Oath of Office" or "Affirmation". ANY "Breach of Contract", which includes and is not, limited to "CIVIL RIGHT" violations – remember the "Bill of Rights" are part of the "Constitution" which is a "CONTRACT" with Americans – these individuals, including the Politicians and any and ALL Corporate Government employees loose the "protection of the government" such as the loss of "Immunity from subject matter", "Immunity from prosecution", Charges-levied against them "Under Breach of Contract", "Authority" and "Jurisdiction" that they think they have against you. In other words, these so-called highly-educated professionals loose what domination they have over you through illegal-practices against you and through "Breach of Contract".

In conclusion, if All American-Civilians were to file a "Notice" or "Put them on Notice" against these Highly-Educated(?) Professional Individuals you may want to consider adding "Breach of Contract" within you Gravamen (Complaint). After all the "Bill of Rights" is/are-our Laws that will put them in check once and for all and are part of the "Constitution-Contract" sworn, autographed and witnessed by those that were elected.

As a Corporation, THE/The/the United States (a corporate government) has and will continue to commit heinous crimes through their "judicial process" against Americans Native/Nationals/Citizens/Civilians. The "judicial process" claims that they process and Try "Facts" on all cases and that all cases are completely different. This is the first notable "Perjury" the Officers of the Courts tell their victims. First of all, the "subject-matter may be different" in each individual case, but the presentation and the 'Rules' they apply before their court system is the same...they operate under Admiralty/Equity/Maritime Jurisdiction (in other words they want the money). In truth it is their burden to produce any and all Contracts against the opposition within the 'subject-matter'.

The UNITED STATES, INC. Court system, as now operated, is UN-Constitutional. Supreme Court Judges and most Court Judges do not take the constitutionally "required"

Oath of Office. These judges commit high crimes and misdemeanors, HIGH-TREASON, R. I. C. O. (Organized Crime Practices), Violation of Sherman Anti-Trust Act (they are a MONOPOLY). Biased, Prejudiced, Union Bar Attorney Judge operates under the law known only to Attorneys and Judges (that work in unison with all of the Banks and Financial Institutions) all for what they think is the "glory" of the all mighty U. S. D. which still is nothing more than a fraud.

The "Court Officers" are already in violation and "Breach of Contract" (by their 'Oath of Office') in their first case. This is how... 1. They offer NO-full disclosures, 2. They tie you into a "Bondage" Contract, 3. Without your knowledge they use your "Birth-Certificate", 4. The "Social-Security" card-number and 5. The "Driver's-License" number. These contracts alone disqualify any and all Judges and Attorneys from representing any case in their "judicial system'. These contracts are commonly referred to as "IMPLIED CONTRACTS" or "Hidden Contracts" and are not enforceable if you can prove they have committed "Breach of Contract"; which is easily done...just not within their 'Courts'. Their attitude is: "Please, come into our Babylonian Court. We want your Labor, Liberty, Property, and Authority over you. We want more fines, taxes, fees, revenue; or we will put you in jail".

Furthermore, to which "Contract" does the Politicians, Judges, Attorneys or any Bureaucrat take the "Oath of Office" for? We all know that there are at least 2 Constitutions that were written in 1700's 1. Was for the development of the government "For the People and by the people" Or 2. The second one that makes everyone into a "Corporate-Entity" through Fraud, Deceit, Trickery, Out Right Lies, Threat, Duress, Coercion?

We, as American-Civilians, can stop this practice by going after those perpetrators with one-single-charge... "Breach of Contract" and hold them responsible for other criminal activities they believe they are "immune from".

The only court that we may be able to proceed with and be heard would be through the International Hague Courts; through a CLASS-ACTION-SUIT. The main reason why is-not only to prove "Breach of Contract" but to charge THE/ The/the UNITED STATES INC. with International War Crimes against American-Civilians and Crimes against Humanity; through the use of Threat, Duress, Coercion and Fraud...just to name a few charges.

The second point for a charge of "Breach of Contract" against these impersonating-self-proclaimed-professionals is the fact that the courts like to use something that is Unconstitutional called 'Administrative-Court-System' or 'Administrative-Hearing"'.

Now here is the problem with using this type system. All legitimate corporations that are in business and have established a D. B. A. (doing business as) within the State Inc. follow their own set of rules known as Policy and Procedures. When an employee commits some sort of wrong or negligence within the company they have what is known as an 'Administrative Hearing'. The internal Investigation makes a decision to terminate or not terminate that employee. It does not matter how large the Corporation is or how small...as an employee you can be terminated for ANY reason, even if it proves to be false.

However, the Corporate Government Inc., especially the socialists tore everything about the idea of a Democracy apart. They were more than taxing one party to the cheers of another in denial of equal protection. It was about creating administrative agencies (1) delegating them to create rules with the force of law as if passed by Congress sanctioned by the people; (2) the creation of administrative courts that defeated the Tripartite (Executive, Legislative and Judicial Branches) government structure usurping all power into the hand of the executive branch, as if this were a dictatorship run by the great hoard of unelected officials.

This type of illegal procedure has been conducted for over 81 years (eighty-one years).

Administrative Law Courts are a fiefdom. They have long been corrupt and traditionally rule in favor of their agencies, making it extremely costly for anyone to even try to defend themselves. If anyone were to attempt to defend themselves they would have the burden of the costs of an Administration proceeding and appeal to an Article III court judge (Oath of Office – Contract or the lack there of... Breach of Contract), then they must appeal to the Court of Appeals, and finally plea to the Supreme Court. Here you will see that there is a chain of evidence and witnesses for a "Breach of Contract" Class-Action-Law-Suit. In truth the cost of such cases are well into the millions of dollars, and then good luck in getting any form of justice.

Furthermore, Administrative Law Courts cannot sentence you to prison, but they can (illegally) fine you into bankruptcy. So the lack of a "criminal prosecution" meant the judges did not have to be lawyers. They could be anyone; brother, sister, brother-in-law etc. etc. who is looking for a job where he/she just rules in favor of the agency not to be bothered with law. Unless the victim has a pile of money, there is no real-chance that they can afford to defend themselves. This is why the agencies cut deals with the "big houses" (courts and banks) and prosecute the small upstarts who lack the funds to defend themselves.

In reality, the Corporate-Government decided that the Administrative Law Courts are really reminiscent of the notorious extrajudicial proceedings of the Star Chamber operated by King James I. The court of Chancery set up outside the King's Bench (so there were no trials by jury), had the same purpose, to circumvent the law. This is where our Fifth Amendment 'Rights' came into being.

The third and final part of the evidence for your Gravamen (Complaint) is that the U. S. Corporate Government Inc. through its "Officials" (elected or not) and all of its subsidiaries (all fifty (50) of them) force you personally into committing a "felonious crime" on a daily basis...this is how they do it:

The Constitution states that all government shall pay for services with gold and/or silver. But yet gives the "government" the right to make coin for the realm...so to speak. However, the Corporate-Government Inc. has decided that it is illegal for anyone to own gold or horde it. So they decided to create a "fictional" monetary system under the Banking system. Instead of individuals paying substance for substance they decided to create a debt-society. For example, if you were to examine a U. S. D. (United States Dollar – such as it is) you will notice across the top of the bill it states "FEDERAL RESERVE NOTE". This paper money actually has no benefit for American-Civilians. In truth you are paying a debt you incur with a debt that they are supplying you with. Furthermore, 'Federal Reserve Notes' you are using are not yours they belong to the "Corporate Government, Inc." and they can come in and take or confiscate any or all of those notes. Why do you think that the National Deficit is so high? We American Civilians cannot pay off a debt with debt.

This is the third piece of evidence to be used against the Judicial Government. Any Corporate Government office or Official that makes a claim you owe them money to their Agency is a fraud. How can you be forced to pay money if you do not have any?

For example, I will explain it this way...We all know who Warren Buffet is and we all know who Donald Trump is...They have made a lot of "MONEY" however, they are no different than you or I... How you ask? They are not "Solvent". They are using the same "debt for debt" bullshit-conscript that everyone else is using.

When the Courts order a victim to pay for restitution, remuneration or damages, those same courts are in control of the Banking System to the point that you will receive nothing or very little if anything...because they absorb it all under trickery, lies and deceit. It's no wonder why that there is "No-Justice"...you cannot buy it, because it does not exist under the debt for debt fraud.

The difference between Trump and Buffet and other members of the Billionaire Boys club and American-Civilians who work on a daily basis for a weekly paycheck, is that they understand how to levy debt against debt. In reality, neither gentlemen actually own anything. They are just as destitute and poor as All American-Civilians; and yes the so-called UNITED STATES Government, Inc. can come and confiscate any and all of their assets under any guise they choose.

Fraud upon the Court is where the Judge (who is NOT the "Court") does NOT support or uphold the Judicial Machinery of the Court. The Court is an unbiased, but methodical "creature" which is governed by the Rule of Law... that is, the Rules of Civil Procedure, the Rules of Criminal Procedure and the Rules of Evidence, all which is overseen by Constitutional law. The Court can only be effective, fair and "just" if it is allowed to function as the laws proscribe. The sad fact is that in most Courts, if not all, across the country, from Federal Courts down to local District courts, have judges who are violating their oath of office and are not properly following these rules, (as most attorney's do not as well, and are usually grossly ignorant of the rules and both judges and attorneys are playing a revised legal-game with their own created rules) and THIS is a Fraud upon the Court, immediately removing jurisdiction from that Court, and vitiates (makes ineffective - invalidates) every decision from that point on. Any judge who does such a thing is under mandatory, non-discretionary duty to recuse himself or herself from the case, and this rarely happens unless someone can force them to do so with the evidence of violations of procedure and threat of losing half their pensions for life which is what can take place. In any case, it is illegal, and EVERY case which has had fraud involved can be re-opened AT ANY TIME, because there are no-statutes of limitations on fraud.

You may be asking yourself who is an "Officer of the Court?" The answer: a judge is an officer of the court, as well as all attorneys. A state judge is a state judicial officer, paid by the federal government to act impartially and lawfully. State and Federal attorneys fall into the same general category and must meet the same requirements. A judge is not the court. People vs. Zajic 88 III. App. 3d. 477, 410 N. E. 2d, 626 (1980).

The definition for "fraud on the court" is as follows: Whenever any officer of the court commits fraud during a proceeding in the court, he/she is engaged in "fraud upon the court"; Bulloch v. United States, 763 F. 2d 1115, 1121 (10th Cir. 1985), the court stated "Fraud upon the court is fraud which is directed to the judicial machinery itself and is not fraud between the parties or fraudulent documents, false statements or perjury. ... It is where the court or a member is corrupted or influenced or influence is attempted or where the judge has not performed his judicial function --- thus where the impartial functions of the court have been directly corrupted."

"Fraud upon the court" has been defined by the 7th Circuit Court of Appeals to "embrace that species of fraud which does, or attempts to, defile the court itself, or is a fraud perpetrated by officers of the court so that the judicial machinery cannot perform in the usual manner its impartial task of adjudging cases that are presented for adjudication." Kenner v. C.I.R., 387 F.3d 689 (1968); 7 Moore's Federal Practice, 2d ed., p. 512, §¶ 60.23. The 7th Circuit further stated "a decision produced by fraud upon the court is not in essence a decision at all, and never becomes final."

What effect does "fraud upon the court" have upon any court proceeding?

"Fraud upon the court" makes void the orders and judgments of that court.

It is also clear and well-settled Illinois law that any attempt to commit "fraud upon the court" vitiates the entire proceeding. The People of the State of Illinois v. Fred E. Sterling, 357 Ill. 354; 192 N.E. 229 (1934) ("The maxim that fraud vitiates every transaction into which it enters applies to judgments as well as to contracts and other transactions."); Allen F. Moore v. Stanley F. Sievers, 336 Ill. 316; 168 N.E. 259 (1929) ("The maxim that fraud vitiates every transaction into which it enters ..."); In re Village of Willowbrook, 37 Ill.App.2d 393 (1962) ("It is axiomatic that fraud vitiates everything."); Dunham v. Dunham, 57 Ill.App. 475 (1894), affirmed 162 Ill. 589 (1896); Skelly Oil Co. v. Universal Oil Products Co., 338 Ill.App. 79, 86 N.E.2d 875, 883-4 (1949); Thomas Stasel v. The American Home Security Corporation, 362 Ill. 350; 199 N.E. 798 (1935).

Under Illinois and Federal law, when any officer of the court has committed "fraud upon the court", the orders and judgment of that court are void, of no legal force or effect.

One of the Remedies for "Breach of Contract" is the 'Disqualifications of Judges'. How do we American-Civilians accomplish this?

Federal law requires the automatic disqualification of a Federal judge under certain circumstances.

In 1994, the U.S. Supreme Court held that "Disqualification is required if an objective observer would entertain reasonable questions about the judge's impartiality. If a judge's attitude or state of mind leads a detached observer to conclude that a fair and impartial hearing is unlikely, the judge must be disqualified." [Emphasis added]. Liteky v. U.S., 114 S. Ct. 1147, 1162 (1994).

Courts have repeatedly held that positive proof of the partiality of a judge is not a requirement, only the appearance of partiality. Liljeberg v. Health Services Acquisition Corp., 486 U.S. 847, 108 S. Ct. 2194 (1988) (what matters is not the reality of bias or prejudice but its appearance); United States v. Balistrieri, 779 F.2d 1191 (7th Cir. 1985) (Section 455(a) "is directed against the appearance of partiality, whether or not the judge is actually biased.") ("Section 455(a) of the Judicial Code, 28 U.S.C. §455(a), is not intended to protect litigants from actual bias in their judge but rather to promote public confidence in the impartiality of the judicial process.").

That Court also stated that Section 455(a) "requires a judge to recuse himself in any proceeding in which her impartiality might reasonably be questioned." Taylor v. O'Grady, 888 F.2d 1189 (7th Cir. 1989). In Pfizer Inc. v. Lord, 456 F.2d 532 (8th Cir. 1972), the Court stated that "It is important that the litigant not only actually receive justice, but that he believes that he has received justice."

The Supreme Court has ruled and has reaffirmed the principle that "justice must satisfy the appearance of justice", Levine v. United States, 362 U.S. 610, 80 S. Ct. 1038 (1960), citing Offutt v. United States, 348 U.S. 11, 14, 75 S. Ct. 11, 13 (1954). A judge receiving a bribe from an interested party over which he is presiding, does not give the appearance of justice.

"Recusal under Section 455 is self-executing; a party need not file affidavits in support of recusal and the judge is obligated to recuse herself sua sponte under the stated circumstances." Taylor v. O'Grady, 888 F.2d 1189(7th Cir. 1989).

Further, the judge has a legal duty to disqualify himself even if there is no motion asking for his disqualification. The Seventh Circuit Court of Appeals further stated that "We think that this language [455(a)] imposes a duty on the judge to act sua sponte, even if no motion or affidavit is filed." Balistrieri, at 1202.

Judges do not have discretion not to disqualify

themselves. By law, they are bound to follow the law. Should a judge not disqualify himself as required by law, then the judge has given another example of his "appearance of partiality" which, possibly, further disqualifies the judge. Should another judge not accept the disqualification of the judge, then the second judge has evidenced an "appearance of partiality" and has possibly disqualified himself/herself. None of the orders issued by any judge who has been disqualified by law would appear to be valid. It would appear that they are void as a matter of law, and are of no legal force or effect.

Should a judge not disqualify himself, then the judge is violation of the Due Process Clause of the U.S. Constitution. United States v. Sciuto, 521 F.2d 842, 845 (7th Cir. 1996) ("The right to a tribunal free from bias or prejudice is based, not on section 144, but on the Due Process Clause.").

Should a judge issue any order after he has been disqualified by law, and if the party has been denied of any of his / her property, then the judge may have been engaged in the Federal Crime of "interference with interstate commerce". The judge has acted in the judge's personal capacity and not in the judge's judicial capacity. It has been said that this judge, acting in this manner, has no more lawful authority than someone's next-door neighbor (provided that he is not a judge). However some judges may not follow the law.

If you were a non-represented litigant, and should the court not follow the law as to non-represented litigants, then the judge has expressed an "appearance of partiality" and, under the law, it would seem that he/she has disqualified him/herself.

However, since not all judges keep up to date in the law, and since not all judges follow the law, it is possible that a judge may not know the ruling of the U.S. Supreme Court and the other courts on this subject. Notice that it states "disqualification is required" and that a judge "must be disqualified" under certain circumstances.

The Supreme Court has also held that if a judge wars against the Constitution, or if he acts without jurisdiction, he has engaged in treason to the Constitution. If a judge acts after he has been automatically disqualified by law, then he is acting without jurisdiction, and that suggest that he is then engaging in criminal acts of treason, and may be engaged in extortion and the interference with interstate commerce.

Courts have repeatedly ruled that judges have no immunity for their criminal acts. Since both treason and the interference with interstate commerce are criminal acts, no judge has immunity to engage in such acts.

However, this also applies those who have taken and "Oath of Office" such as the Politicians – who claim they have no 'authority to get involved with (other) STATE BUSINESS or (other) COURT PROCEEDINGS. This is misinformation they are giving you, remember they took an oath to support and defend the "CONSTITUTION" of the United States from 'Foreign and Domestic'. If they refuse to help or guide you they now become by definition 'accomplices after the fact'. It is like when a bank robber or bank robbers go into a bank and rob it...the get-away driver is NOT in the bank but in a parking lot...Why then, does the Driver receive MORE years as opposed to those who actually robbed the Bank? This question is not trying to mix apple and oranges, but to prove a point...and I do believe I made it.

Furthermore, if any "Public-Servant" abuses their authority or makes "False-Claims" against an American-Civilian they need to be brought up on charges of "Breach of Contract" and if they are found 'guilty' they lose their pensions and retirement with the exception of their Social Security income.

Chapter 4

A REMEDY FOR "BREACH OF CONTRACT" WITH EXAMPLES FROM POLITICIANS

First, we wish to thank all of the States that contributed for this chapter. For those States that refused to honor a written-request for the Oath/Affirmation from their Governor's, Lt. Governor's, Secretary of State, and State Attorney General you do your State a dis-service by hiding your "Breach of Contract"; which is tantamount to Obstruct Justice and High Treason.

This chapter is dedicated for the evidence of the basic contracts that apply to all elected Officials from the Presidency to the State Officials. These are actual "contracts" from individuals who have been elected or appointed. These "contracts" are presented to you in alphabetical order for your convenience starting with the Presidential Oath of Office followed by individual States Oaths/Affirmations from individual State Elected/Appointed Officials. We wish to thank all of the States that were kind enough to supply us with these contracts, even though some of them were paid for...not problem there.

However, those states that refused to comply...well we know you are trying to hide something or you just "think you are above the law" and that "contracts" do not apply to you...Big mistake!!

We have received responses from the States, Inc. for examples of their contracts and "Breach of Contract" for those who did NOT respond.

Each contract within this book is from 2, 4 or 6 year terms. Unless specified or they are bureaucrats under those Political-Corporate-Whores who are under said "Oath of Office" and are responsible for the Bureaucratic/Employee actions and decisions 'good' or 'bad'. The "Elected-Official's" are responsible for those decisions that hurt American-Civilians who cannot "afford" to have 'representation' at their expense. The Government Employees are set out to-commit crimes against American-Civilians for the all mighty dollar; if you doubt this look up the definition of "color of law". If you do not think that this is a "CONSPIRACY" try defending yourself against ANY and all of the AGENCIES.

We will start with the first two-contracts known as the "The Constitution" and the "Bill of Rights". Then show the contracts which have been sign[ed]/autograph[ed] by those in-office (Incumbents) and those that have been elected into office (for the first-time) and their Subsidiaries (which include all States, Inc. Counties, Inc. and Cities, Inc.).

The "Constitution of the united States of America" was autographed by 39 members on September 17, 1787. This "contract" set Limits and Prohibitions against what the Corporate-Government, Inc. could do to "Individual-American-Civilians", or the 'PEOPLE'.

The "Bill of Rights" was accepted and the effective date was December 15, 1791. This "contract" was established as the "First ten Amendments" for the Constitution and directly protects Individual-American-Civilians and their "Rights".

However, there is one "contract" that supersedes the above named contracts...that contract is actually called a "Covenant" and is known as the Ten Commandments; which were written by "The Finger of GOD".

However, there is a Remedy that can and will cure some of the "illegal" practices against American-Civilians. The first-step though is to prove through their paperwork a "Breach of Contract". After proof of any "Breach of Contract" has been established we as Americans can establish what is called a "CLASS-ACTION-SUIT" and have the perpetrators removed from Office and kept from doing any-more-harm. When the "Breach of Contract" has been established the parties that have committed violations against American-Civilians can then be charged with other crimes such as: Fraud, Extortion, Racketeering under R. I. C. O. and War Crimes against American-Civilians. By the/a "Breach of Contract" if and when it has been established, the perpetrators such as judges, lawyers, police, bureaucrats even politicians lose all of the 'immunities' that they are awarded when they campaign for public-office and would also include 'subject-matter' for judges and other court officers.

Any violation of any Americans'-Civil-Rights constitutes a "Breach of Contract". Notice that it does not say "Privileges" but Civil Rights.

Here are some fine examples for "Breach of Contract" by using the "Sworn Oath of Office" from Governors, Lt. Governors, State Attorney Generals, and Secretary of States. Remember these are 'authentic' Con-tracts and are legal and binding for those perpetrators who are employed by each different subsidiary of THE/The/the united States of America.

The Constitution

We the People

of the United States, in Order to form a more perfect Union, establish Justice, insure domestic Tranquility, provide for the common Defence, promote the general Welfare, and secure the Blessings of Liberty to ourselves and our Posterity, do ordain and establish this CONSTITUTION for the United States of America.

Article I.

SECTION 1. All legislative Powers herein granted shall be vested in a Congress of the United States, which shall consist of a Senate and House of Representatives.

SECTION 2. The House of Representatives shall be composed of Members chosen every second Year by the People of the several States, and the Electors in each State shall have the Qualifications requisite for Electors of the most numerous Branch of the State Legislature.

No Person shall be a Representative who shall not have attained to the Age of twenty-five Years, and been seven Years a Citizen of the United States, and who shall not, when elected, be an Inhabitant of that State in which he shall be chosen.

[Representatives and direct Taxes shall be apportioned among the several States which may be included within this Union, according to their respective Numbers, which shall be determined by adding to the whole Number of free Persons, including those bound to Service for a Term of Years, and excluding Indians not taxed, three fifths of all other Persons.] The actual Enumeration shall be made within three Years after the first Meeting of the Congress of the United States, and within every subsequent Term of ten Years, in such Manner as they shall by Law direct. The Number of Representatives shall not exceed one for every thirty Thousand, but each State shall have at Least one Representative; and until such enumeration shall be made, the State of New Hampshire shall be entitled to chuse three, Massachusetts eight, Rhode-Island and Providence Plantations one, Connecticut five, New-York six, New Jersey four, Pennsylvania eight, Delaware one, Maryland six, Virginia ten, North Carolina five, South Carolina five, and Georgia three.

When vacancies happen in the Representation from any State, the Executive Authority thereof shall issue Writs of Election to fill such Vacancies.

The House of Representatives shall chuse their Speaker and other Officers; and shall have the sole Power of Impeachment.

SECTION 3. The Senate of the United States shall be composed of two Senators from each State, chosen by the Legislature thereof, for six Years; and each Senator shall have one Vote.

Immediately after they shall be assembled in Consequence of the first Election, they shall be divided as equally as may be into three Classes. The Seats of the Senators of the first Class shall be vacated at the Expiration of the second Year, of the second Class at the Expiration of the fourth Year, and of the third Class at the Expiration of the sixth Year, so that one-third may be chosen every second Year; and if Vacancies happen by Resignation, or otherwise, during the Recess of the Legislature of any State, the Executive thereof may make temporary Appointments until the next Meeting of the Legislature, which shall then fill such Vacancies.

No Person shall be a Senator who shall not have attained to the Age of thirty Years, and been nine Years a Citizen of the United States, and who shall not, when elected, be an Inhabitant of that State for which he shall be chosen.

The Vice President of the United States shall be President of the Senate, but shall have no Vote, unless they be equally divided.

The Senate shall chuse their other Officers, and also a President pro tempore, in the absence of the Vice President, or when he shall exercise the Office of President of the United States.

The Senate shall have the sole Power to try all Impeachments. When sitting for that Purpose, they shall be on Oath or Affirmation. When the President of the United States is tried, the Chief Justice shall preside: And no Person shall be convicted without the Concurrence of two thirds of the Members present.

Judgment in Cases of Impeachment shall not extend further than to removal from Office, and disqualification to hold and enjoy any Office of honor, Trust or Profit under the United States: but the Party convicted shall nevertheless be liable and subject to Indictment, Trial, Judgment and Punishment, according to Law.

Bill of Rights

Congress of the United States,
begun and held at the City of New-York, on
Wednesday, the fourth of March, one thousand seven hundred and eighty nine.

Presidential Oath of Office

Please note: The following Documents are from original documents. However, the individual that signed/autographed the document(s) may or may not be in office. Furthermore, the "contracts" are still in full effect no matter who signs or autographs them or newly elected or re-elected as an incumbent.

We wish to thank the Jimmy Carter Presidential Library Museum in Georgia for their contribution of his "Oath of Office".

The American Presidency Project

JIMMY CARTER

A's

Alabama

Alaska

Arizona

Arkansas

Oath of Office

I, Robert Bentley, solemnly swear that I will support the Constitution of the United States, and the Constitution of the State of Alabama, so long as I continue a citizen thereof; and that I will faithfully and honestly discharge the duties of the office upon which I am about to enter, to the best of my ability. So help me God.

Signed on this 19th day of January, 2015.

Robert Bentley

Robert Bentley
Governor

Sworn to and subscribed before me on this 19th day of January, 2015.

Roy Moore

Roy S. Moore
Chief Justice, Alabama Supreme Court

Lt. Governor Kay Ivey
Oath of Office

STATE OF ALABAMA)

MONTGOMERY COUNTY)

I, Kay Ivey, solemnly swear that I will support the Constitution of the United States, and the Constitution of the State of Alabama, so long as I continue a citizen thereof; and that I will faithfully and honestly discharge the duties of the office upon which I am about to enter, to the best of my ability. So help me God.

_____ L.S.
Kay Ivey - Lt. Governor

SWORN TO AND SUBSCRIBED before me this the 19th day of January, 2015.

_____
William B. Sellers
Notary Public
State of Alabama At-Large

My commission expires: August 29, 2016

2137521

Flag of the United States of the America
Title: 4: U.S.A. Codex: Chapter: 1: Section: 182

Oath of Office

I, _____ John Harold Merrill _____ solemnly swear (or affirm, as the case may be) that I will support the Constitution of the United States, and the Constitution of the State of Alabama, so long as I continue a citizen thereof; and that I will faithfully and honestly discharge the duties of the office upon which I am about to enter, to the best of my ability, So help me God.

_____
Signature

Alabama Secretary of State
_____
Office

Certification of Administering Officer

The above Oath was subscribed and sworn to before me this
_____ 19th _____ day of January _____ 2015 _____

_____
Signature of Administering Officer

Notary Public
_____
Title

Horace S. Merrill
My Comp   tion Expires
9-24-207

92

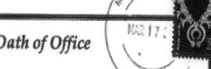

Oath of Office

I, **Luther Johnson Strange, III,** *solemnly swear that I will support the Constitution of the United States, and the Constitution of the State of Alabama, so long as I continue a citizen thereof; and that I will faithfully and honestly discharge the duties of the office upon which I am about to enter, to the best of my ability. So help me God.*

Luther Johnson Strange

Luther Johnson Strange, III - Signature

ATTORNEY GENERAL

Office

Certification of Administering Officer

The above Oath was subscribed and sworn to before me this Nineteenth day of January 2015.

William H. Pryor Jr. - Signature of Administering Officer

JUDGE OF THE UNITED STATES COURT OF APPEALS
FOR THE ELEVENTH CIRCUIT

Title

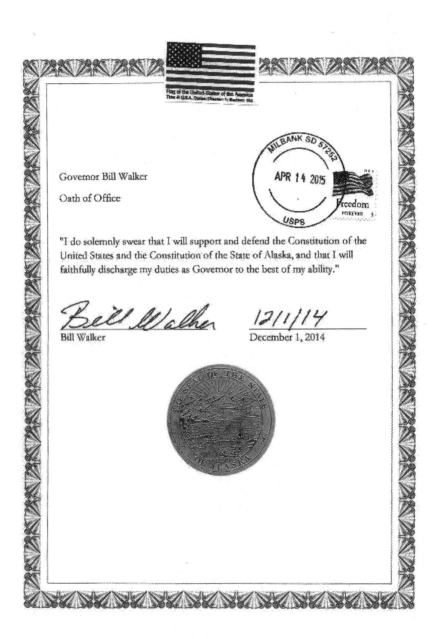

Governor Bill Walker

Oath of Office

"I do solemnly swear that I will support and defend the Constitution of the United States and the Constitution of the State of Alaska, and that I will faithfully discharge my duties as Governor to the best of my ability."

Bill Walker

December 1, 2014

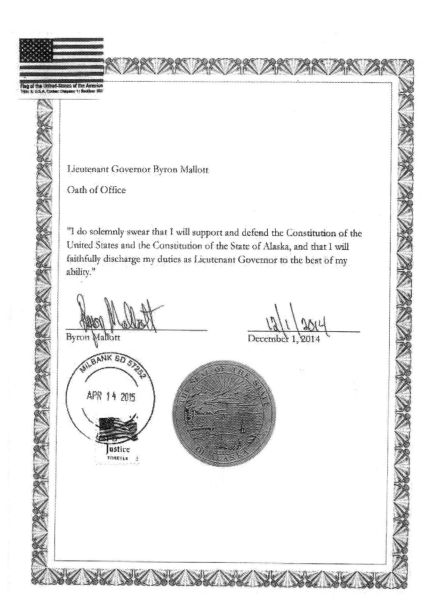

Lieutenant Governor Byron Mallott

Oath of Office

"I do solemnly swear that I will support and defend the Constitution of the
United States and the Constitution of the State of Alaska, and that I will
faithfully discharge my duties as Lieutenant Governor to the best of my
ability."

_____
Byron Mallott

_____
December 1, 2014

95

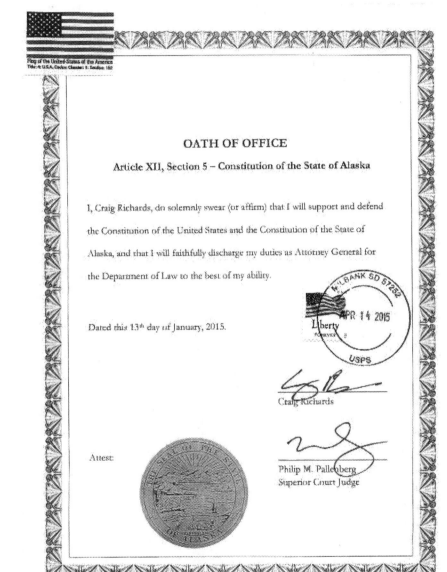

OATH OF OFFICE

Article XII, Section 5 – Constitution of the State of Alaska

I, Craig Richards, do solemnly swear (or affirm) that I will support and defend the Constitution of the United States and the Constitution of the State of Alaska, and that I will faithfully discharge my duties as Attorney General for the Department of Law to the best of my ability.

Dated this 13th day of January, 2015.

_____
Craig Richards

Attest:

_____
Philip M. Pallenberg
Superior Court Judge

Loyalty Oath of Office

State of Arizona

County of Maricopa

I, Janice K. Brewer, do solemnly swear that I will support the Constitution of the United States and the Constitution and laws of the State of Arizona; that I will bear true faith and allegiance to the same, and defend them against all enemies, foreign and domestic, and that I will faithfully and impartially discharge the duties of the office of Governor according to the best of my ability, so help me God.

Honorable Janice K. Brewer

Oath Administered By:

Honorable Rebecca White Berch
Chief Justice, Arizona Supreme Court

Oath Witnessed By:

Michael Wilford Brewer
Attorney at Law

Dr. John Brewer

Filed in the Office of the Secretary of State on this 3rd day of January, 2011 at 2:41 p.m.

Ken Bennett
Secretary of State

Loyalty Oath of Office

State of Arizona

County of Maricopa

    I, Ken Bennett, do solemnly swear that I will support the Constitution of the United States and the Constitution and laws of the State of Arizona; that I will bear true faith and allegiance to the same, and defend them against all enemies, foreign and domestic, and that I will faithfully and impartially discharge the duties of the office of Secretary of State according to the best of my ability, so help me God.

Honorable Ken Bennett

Oath Administered By:

Honorable Rebecca White Berch
Chief Justice, Arizona Supreme Court

Oath Witnessed By:

Jeanne Bennett

Filed in the Office of the Secretary of State on this 3rd day of January, 2011 at 2:41 ,p.m.

Ken Bennett
Secretary of State

98

Loyalty Oath of Office

State of Arizona

County of Maricopa

    I, Tom Horne, do solemnly swear that I will support the Constitution of the United States and the Constitution and laws of the State of Arizona; that I will bear true faith and allegiance to the same, and defend them against all enemies, foreign and domestic, and that I will faithfully and impartially discharge the duties of the office of Attorney General according to the best of my ability, so help me God.

_____
Honorable Tom Horne

Oath Administered By:

_____
Honorable Rebecca White Berch
Chief Justice, Arizona Supreme Court

Filed in the Office of the Secretary of State on this 3rd day of January, 2011 at 2 : 41 ,p.m.

_____
Ken Bennett
Secretary of State

99

State of Arkansas

Flag of the United States of the America
Title: 4: U.S.A. Codex: Chapter: 1: Section: 182

Duplicate Official Oath of Office

Every officer administering this Oath of Office is required by law to endorse this duplicate thereof, which must be returned to the Secretary of State, State Capitol, Room 026, Little Rock, Arkansas, 72201, **WITHIN FIFTEEN (15) DAYS** *after the Commission is dated.*

I, Mike Beebe, do solemnly swear (or affirm) that I will support the Constitution of the United States and the Constitution of the State of Arkansas, and that I will faithfully discharge the duties of the office of Governor, upon which I am about to enter.

_____
(signature)

1800 Center Street
(street address)

L R   72206
(city, state, zip code)

501 682 2345
(telephone number)

Sworn to and subscribed before me, _Jim Hannah_
(name of person administering oath)

A _Chief Justice_ in and for the _Supreme Court of Arkansas_
(position of administering officer)   (state, county, or judicial district)

this __11th__ day of _January_ , 201_1_.

_____
(signature of Administering Officer)

This Oath may be administered through the provisions of ACA 21-2-105 depending on the office to which you were elected but
NOT BY A NOTARY PUBLIC!**

State of Arkansas

Duplicate Official Oath of Office

Every officer administering this Oath of Office is required by law to endorse this duplicate thereof, which must be returned to the Secretary of State, State Capitol, Room 026, Little Rock, Arkansas, 72201, **WITHIN FIFTEEN (15) DAYS** *after the Commission is dated.*

I, Mark Alan Darr, do solemnly swear (or affirm) that I will support the Constitution of the United States and the Constitution of the State of Arkansas, and that I will faithfully discharge the duties of the office of Lieutenant Governor, upon which I am about to enter.

_____
(signature)

4031 PASOFINO LOOP
(street address)

Springdale, AR 72764
(city, state, zip code)

501-607-3277
(telephone number)

Sworn to and subscribed before me, __Jim Hannah__
(name of person administering oath)

A __Chief Justice__ in and for the __Supreme Court of Arkansas__
(position of administering officer) (state, county, or judicial district)

this __11th__ day of __January__ , 201_1_ .

_____
(signature of Administering Officer)

This Oath may be administered through the provisions of ACA 21-2-105 depending on the office to which you were elected but **NOT BY A NOTARY PUBLIC!**

State of Arkansas

Duplicate Official Oath of Office

Every officer administering this Oath of Office is required by law to endorse this duplicate thereof, which must be returned to the Secretary of State, State Capitol, Room 026, Little Rock, Arkansas, 72201, **WITHIN FIFTEEN (15) DAYS** *after the Commission is dated.*

I, Mark Martin, do solemnly swear (or affirm) that I will support the Constitution of the United States and the Constitution of the State of Arkansas, and that I will faithfully discharge the duties of the office of Secretary of State, upon which I am about to enter.

Mark Martin
(signature)

FILED

JAN 12 2011

CHARLIE DANIELS
SECRETARY OF STATE

123 North Pittman Street
(street address)

Prairie Grove, Arkansas 72753
(city, state, zip code)

479-846-1889
(telephone number)

Sworn to and subscribed before me, __Jim Hannah__
(name of person administering oath)

A __Chief Justice__ in and for the __Supreme Court of Arkansas__
(position of administering officer)   (state, county, or judicial district)

this __11th__ day of __January__, 201_1_.

Jim Hannah
(signature of Administering Officer)

This Oath may be administered through the provisions of ACA 21-2-105 depending on the office to which you were elected but **NOT BY A NOTARY PUBLIC!**

State of Arkansas

Duplicate Official Oath of Office

Every officer administering this Oath of Office is required by law to endorse this duplicate thereof, which must be returned to the Secretary of State, State Capitol, Room 026, Little Rock, Arkansas, 72201, **WITHIN FIFTEEN (15) DAYS** *after the Commission is dated.*

I, Dustin McDaniel, do solemnly swear (or affirm) that I will support the Constitution of the United States and the Constitution of the State of Arkansas, and that I will faithfully discharge the duties of the office of Attorney General, upon which I am about to enter.

(signature)

323 Center Street, Suite 200
(street address)

Little Rock AR 72201
(city, state, zip code)

(501) 682-2427
(telephone number)

FILED
JAN 1 . 2011
CHARLIE DANIELS
SECRETARY OF STATE

Sworn to and subscribed before me, __Jim Hannah__
(name of person administering oath)

A __Chief Justice__ in and for the __Supreme Court of Arkansas__
(position of administering officer)   (state, county, or judicial district)

this ___11th___ day of ___January___, 2011.

(signature of Administering Officer)

This Oath may be administered through the provisions of ACA 21-2-105 depending on the office to which you were elected but
NOT BY A NOTARY PUBLIC!

103

C's

California

Colorado

Connecticut

STATE OF CALIFORNIA

GOVERNOR EDMUND G. BROWN JR.

OATH

for the Office of ___Governor of the State of California___

I, ___Edmund G. Brown Jr.___, *do solemnly swear (or affirm) that I will support and defend the Constitution of the United States and the Constitution of the State of California against all enemies, foreign and domestic; that I will bear true faith and allegiance to the Constitution of the United States and the Constitution of the State of California; that I take this obligation freely, without any mental reservation or purpose of evasion; and that I will well and faithfully discharge the duties upon which I am about to enter.*

Signature ___[signature: Edmund G. Brown Jr.]___

Term Expires ___January 4, 2015___

Subscribed and sworn to before me,
this __3rd__ *day of* __January__
A. D. __2011__

___[signature]___
Chief Justice of the Supreme Court

STATE CAPITOL • SACRAMENTO, CALIFORNIA 95814

105

FILED
in the office of the Secretary of State
of the State of California

JAN – 4 2011

By _SLGustagua_
Deputy Secretary of State

OATH

For the Office of Secretary of State

I, Debra Bowen, solemnly swear (or affirm) that I will support and defend the Constitution of the United States and the Constitution of the State of California against all enemies, foreign and domestic; that I will bear true faith and allegiance to the Constitution of the United States and the Constitution of the State of California; that I take this obligation freely, without any mental reservation or purpose of evasion; and that I will well and faithfully discharge the duties upon which I am about to enter.

Signature _____

Subscribed and sworn to before me,
Kamala Harris, Attorney General

this __4th__ day of __January__

AD __2011__

Signature _____

FILED
In the office of the Secretary of State
of the State of California

JAN 2 2 2015

By _____
Deputy Secretary of State

OATH

For the Office of Attorney General of the State of California

I, <u>Kamala D. Harris</u>, do solemnly swear (or affirm) that I will support and defend the Constitution of the United States and the Constitution of the State of California against all enemies, foreign and domestic; that I will bear true faith and allegiance to the Constitution of the United States and the Constitution of the State of California; that I take this obligation freely, without any mental reservation or purpose of evasion; and that I will well and faithfully discharge the duties upon which I am about to enter.

Signature

Subscribed and sworn to before me,
this 5th day of January, A.D. 2015

Honorable Tani Cantil-Sakauye
Chief Justice of the California Supreme Court

107

STATE OF COLORADO

GOVERNOR
OATH OF OFFICE

I, John W. Hickenlooper, do solemnly swear by the everliving God, that I will support the Constitution of the United States and of the State of Colorado, and faithfully perform the duties of the office of Governor of State of the State of Colorado, to which I am about to enter.

Subscribed and sworn to before me this
Eleventh Day of January A.D. 2011

Honorable Michael Bender
Chief Justice, Colorado Supreme Court

108

STATE OF COLORADO

20115000871 C
OATH_OFFICE
SECRETARY OF STATE
1/13/2011 02:40:46

LIEUTENANT GOVERNOR
OATH OF OFFICE

I, Joseph A. Garcia, do solemnly swear by the everliving God, that I will support the Constitution of the United States and of the State of Colorado, and faithfully perform the duties of the office of Lieutenant Governor of the State of Colorado, to which I am about to enter.

Subscribed and sworn to before me this
Eleventh Day of January A.D. 2011

Honorable Michael Bender
Chief Justice, Colorado Supreme Court

109

STATE OF COLORADO

DEC 26 2014

SECRETARY OF STATE
OATH OF OFFICE

I, Scott Gessler, do solemnly swear by the everliving God, that I will support the Constitution of the United States and of the State of Colorado, and faithfully perform the duties of the office of Secretary of State of the State of Colorado, to which I am about to enter.

Subscribed and sworn to before me this Eleventh Day of January A.D. 2011

Honorable Michael Bender
Chief Justice, Colorado Supreme Court

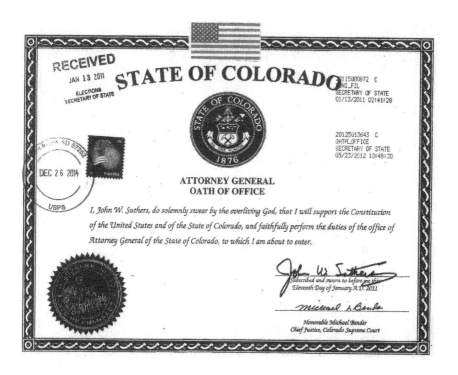

STATE OF COLORADO

20115000872 C
WI_FIL
SECRETARY OF STATE
01/13/2011 02:41:28

20125013643 C
OATH_OFFICE
SECRETARY OF STATE
05/23/2012 10:48:30

DEC 26 2014

USPS

ATTORNEY GENERAL
OATH OF OFFICE

I, John W. Suthers, do solemnly swear by the everliving God, that I will support the Constitution of the United States and of the State of Colorado, and faithfully perform the duties of the office of Attorney General of the State of Colorado, to which I am about to enter.

John W. Suthers

Subscribed and sworn to before me this
Eleventh Day of January A.D. 2011

Michael L Bender

Honorable Michael Bender
Chief Justice, Colorado Supreme Court

111

The State of Connecticut refused to reply upon our request for copies of the Oath/Affirmation of their Elected Officials.

However the Elected Officials, by **Law**, are required to Sign/Autograph the Oath/Affirmation of Office.

The omittance of these documents is tantamount to "Breach of Contract" and "Obstruction of Justice".

D

Delaware

Feb. 25. 2015 5:18PM
State of Delaware
1429 Longworth House Office Building
(302) 229-1165; 229-1291
Washington: (302) 456-0900
Web Site

Flag of the United States of the America
Title: 4: U.S.A. Codes: Chapter: 3: Section: 1A2

ARTICLE XIV.

OATH OF OFFICE

§1. Form of oath for members of General Assembly and public officers.

Members of the General Assembly and all public officers executive and judicial, except such inferior officers as shall be by law exempted, shall, before they enter upon the duties of their respected offices, take and subscribe the following oath or affirmation:

"I, _____(name),_____ do proudly swear (or affirm) to carry out the responsibilities of the office of ___(name of office)_____ to the best of my ability, freely acknowledging that the powers of this office flow from the people I am privileged to represent. I further swear (or affirm) always to place the public interest above any special or personal interests, and to respect the right of future generations to share the rich historic and natural heritage of Delaware. In doing so I will always uphold and defend the Constitutions of my Country and my State, so help me God."

No other oath, declaration or test shall be required as a qualification for any office of public trust.

114

F

Florida

Flag of the United States of the People
Title 4, U.S.A. Code, Chapter 1, Section 1&2

OATH OF OFFICE
(Art. II, § 5(b), Fla. Const.)

STATE OF FLORIDA

County of Leon

I do solemnly swear (or affirm) that I will support, protect, and defend the Constitution and Government of the United States and of the State of Florida; that I am duly qualified to hold office under the Constitution of the State, and that I will well and faithfully perform the duties of

Governor
(Title of Office)

on which I am now about to enter, so help me God.

[NOTE: If you affirm, you may omit the words "so help me God." *See* § 92.52, Fla. Stat.]

_____
Signature

Sworn to and subscribed before me this 2nd day of JANUARY, 2015

Diane Moulton
Signature of Officer Administering Oath

DIANE MOULTON
MY COMMISSION # FF 026957
EXPIRES October 18, 2017
Bonded Thru Notary Public Underwriters

_____
Print, Type, or Stamp Commissioned Name of Notary Public

Personally Known ☒ OR Produced Identification ☐

Type of Identification Produced _____

MAR 19 2015
USPS

- -

ACCEPTANCE

I accept the office listed in the above Oath of Office.

Mailing Address: ☒ Home ☐ Office

700 NORTH ADAMS ST
Street or Post Office Box

RICK SCOTT
Print name as you desire commission issued

TALL, FL 32303
City, State, Zip Code

_____
Signature

DS-DE 56 (Rev. 02/10)

116

OATH OF OFFICE
(Art. II. § 5(b), Fla. Const.)

STATE OF FLORIDA

County of Leon

I do solemnly swear (or affirm) that I will support, protect, and defend the Constitution and Government of the United States and of the State of Florida; that I am duly qualified to hold office under the Constitution of the State, and that I will well and faithfully perform the duties of

Lieutenant Governor
_____
(Title of Office)

on which I am now about to enter, so help me God.

[NOTE: If you affirm, you may omit the words "so help me God." See § 92.52, Fla. Stat.]

_____
Signature

Sworn to and subscribed before me this 5 day of January 15

_____
Signature of Officer Administering Oath or of Notary Public

Jennifer L. Pease
_____
Print, Type, or Stamp Commissioned Name of Notary Public

Personally Known ☒ OR Produced Identification ☐

_____
Type of Identification Produced

- -

ACCEPTANCE

I accept the office listed in the above Oath of Office.

Mailing Address: ☐ Home ☒ Office

400 S. Monroe St, PL-05
Street or Post Office Box

Tallahassee, FL 32399
City, State, Zip Code

CARLOS LOPEZ-CANTERA
Print name as you desire commission issued

_____
Signature

DS-DE 56 (Rev. 02/10)

117

OATH OF OFFICE
(Art. II. § 5(b), Fla. Const.)

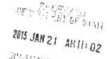

STATE OF FLORIDA

County of _____Leon_____

I do solemnly swear (or affirm) that I will support, protect, and defend the Constitution and Government of the United States and of the State of Florida; that I am duly qualified to hold office under the Constitution of the State, and that I will well and faithfully perform the duties of

_____Secretary of State_____
(Title of Office)

on which I am now about to enter, so help me God.

[NOTE: If you affirm, you may omit the words "so help me God." *See* § 92.52, Fla. Stat.]

_____
Signature

Sworn to and subscribed before me this 21 day of January 15

_____
Signature of Officer Administering Oath or of Notary Public

_____
Print, Type, or Stamp Commissioned Name of Notary Public

Personally Known ☒ OR   Produced Identification ☐

Type of Identification Produced _____

ACCEPTANCE

I accept the office listed in the above Oath of Office.

Mailing Address: ☐ Home ☒ Office

_____500 So Bronough_____
Street or Post Office Box

_____Tallahassee, Florida_____
City, State, Zip Code   32399

_____Ken Detzner_____
Print name as you desire commission issued

_____
Signature

DS-DE 56 (Rev, 02/10)

OATH OF OFFICE

(Art. II. § 5(b), Fla. Const.)

RECEIVED
DEPARTMENT OF STATE

2014 DEC 12 AM 10: 24

DIVISION OF ELECTIONS
TALLAHASSEE, FL

STATE OF FLORIDA

County of Leon

I do solemnly swear (or affirm) that I will support, protect, and defend the Constitution and Government of the United States and of the State of Florida; that I am duly qualified to hold office under the Constitution of the State, and that I will well and faithfully perform the duties of

Attorney General - Florida

(Title of Office)

on which I am now about to enter, so help me God.

[NOTE: If you affirm, you may omit the words "so help me God." See § 92.52, Fla. Stat.]

Signature

Sworn to and subscribed before me this 9 day of DECEMBER, 2014.

Signature of Officer Administering Oath or of Notary Public

Print, Type, or Stamp Commissioned Name of Notary Public.

Personally Known ☑ OR

ELIZABETH BENNETT WHITLEY
Notification: SION #FF172464
EXPIRES October 29, 2018

Type of Identification Produced _____

ACCEPTANCE

I accept the office listed in the above Oath of Office.

Mailing Address: ☐ Home ☑ Office

The Capitol PL-01

Street or Post Office Box

Tallahassee, FL 32399-1050

City, State, Zip Code

Pam Bondi

Print name as you desire commission issued

Signature

OATH OF OFFICE
(Art. II. § 5(b), Fla. Const.)

STATE OF FLORIDA

County of __Leon__

I do solemnly swear (or affirm) that I will support, protect, and defend the Constitution and Government of the United States and of the State of Florida; that I am duly qualified to hold office under the Constitution of the State, and that I will well and faithfully perform the duties of

__Chief Financial Officer__
(Title of Office)

on which I am now about to enter, so help me God.

[NOTE: If you affirm, you may omit the words "so help me God." *See* § 92.52, Fla. Stat.]

Signature _____

Sworn to and subscribed before me this __13th__ day of __January__, __2015__.

Signature of Officer _____

Commission # FP 081644
Expires January 24, 2018

Print, Type, or Stamp _____

Personally Known ☑ OR   Produced Identification ☐

Type of Identification Produced _____

- -

ACCEPTANCE

I accept the office listed in the above Oath of Office.

Mailing Address: ☐ Home ☑ Office

__400 S. Monroe St, PL 11__
Street or Post Office Box __The Capitol__

__Tallahassee, FL 32399__
City, State, Zip Code

__Jeffrey H. Atwater__
Print name as you desire commission issued

Signature _____

DS-DE 56 (Rev. 02/10)

120

OATH OF OFFICE
(Art. II. § 5(b), Fla. Const.)

STATE OF FLORIDA

County of Leon

I do solemnly swear (or affirm) that I will support, protect, and defend the Constitution and Government of the United States and of the State of Florida; that I am duly qualified to hold office under the Constitution of the State, and that I will well and faithfully perform the duties of

Commissioner of Agriculture
(Title of Office)

on which I am now about to enter, so help me God.

[NOTE: If you affirm, you may omit the words "so help me God." *See* § 92.52, Fla. Stat.]

_____
Signature

Sworn to and subscribed before me this 9th day of November , 2014

_____
Signature of Officer Administering Oath or of Notary Public

WENDY L. EVANS
Notary Public - State of Florida
My Comm. Expires Aug 7, 2018
Commission # FF 112638

_____
Print, Type, or Stamp Commissioned Name of Notary Public

Personally Known ☒   OR   Produced Identification ☐

Type of Identification Produced _____

- -

ACCEPTANCE

I accept the office listed in the above Oath of Office.

Mailing Address: ☐ Home   ☒ Office

400 S. Monroe Street, The Capitol PL-10
Street or Post Office Box

Tallahassee, Florida 32399
City, State, Zip Code

Adam H. Putnam
Print name as you desire commission issued

_____
Signature

DS-DE 56 (Rev. 02/10)

G

Georgia

FEB 17 2015
ELECTIONS DIVISION

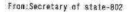

OFFICIAL OATH OF GOVERNOR
STATE OF GEORGIA

STATE OF GEORGIA
COUNTY OF FULTON

I, *Nathan Deal*, do solemnly swear (or affirm) that I will faithfully execute the office of *Governor of the State of Georgia* and will, to the best of my ability, preserve, protect, and defend the Constitution thereof and the Constitution of the United States.

> I do further solemnly swear (or affirm) that I am not the holder of any unaccounted for public money due this State, or any political subdivision or authority thereof; that I am not the holder of any office of trust under the government of the United States, any other state, or any foreign state which I am prohibited from holding by the laws of the State of Georgia, and that I am otherwise qualified to hold said office, according to the Constitution of the United States and Laws of Georgia; and that I will support the Constitutions of the United States and of this State.

SO HELP ME GOD!

Sworn to and subscribed before me this
....*14*..day of...*January*........20*15*.

THE HONORABLE JASON J. DEAL
Superior Court Judge
Northeastern Judicial Circuit

.............*Nathan Deal*............
Signature

123

H

Hawaii

The State of Hawaii refused to reply upon our request for copies of the Oath/Affirmation of their Elected Officials.

However the Elected Officials, by **Law**, are required to Sign/Autograph the Oath/Affirmation of Office.

The omittance of these documents is tantamount to "Breach of Contract" and "Obstruction of Justice".

I's

Idaho
Illinois
Indiana
Iowa

OFFICIAL OATH

I do solemnly swear (or affirm, as the case may be) that I will support the Constitution of the United States, and the Constitution of the State of Idaho, and that I will faithfully

discharge the duties of (insert office) __OFFICE OF THE GOVERNOR, STATE OF IDAHO__

according to the best of my ability.

C. L. "BUTCH" OTTER

Subscribed and sworn to before me this __5__ day of __January__, __2015__

Notary Public for the State of Idaho

US District Judge

Commission Expires

J Felter, Notary
commission Exp. aug 19, 2019

127

OFFICIAL OATH

2015 JAN -5 AM ID: 49

SECRETARY OF STATE
STATE OF IDAHO

I do solemnly swear (or affirm, as the case may be) that I will support the Constitution of

the United States, and the Constitution of the State of Idaho, and that I will faithfully

discharge the duties of (insert office) __LIEUTENANT GOVERNOR, STATE OF IDAHO__

according to the best of my ability, *So help me God*

BRAD LITTLE

Subscribed and sworn to before me this __5th__ day of __January__, __2015__

_____, David W. Gent
Notary Public for the State of Idaho
Hon. Judge of Idaho Court of Appeals
_____
Commission Expires

Rev. 08/2000

OFFICIAL OATH

I do solemnly swear (or affirm, as the case may be) that I will support the Constitution of

the United States, and the Constitution of the State of Idaho, and that I will faithfully

discharge the duties of (insert office)   SECRETARY OF STATE, STATE OF IDAHO

according to the best of my ability.

LAWERENCE E. DENNEY

Subscribed and sworn to before me this 5 day of January 2015

Notary Public for the State of Idaho

Justice Idaho Supreme Court
Commission Expires

Rev. 08/2000

129

OFFICIAL OATH

I do solemnly swear (or affirm, as the case may be) that I will support the Constitution of

the United States, and the Constitution of the State of Idaho, and that I will faithfully

discharge the duties of (insert office) _____ ATTORNEY GENERAL, STATE OF IDAHO

_____

according to the best of my ability.

LAWRENCE WASDEN

Subscribed and sworn to before me this 22nd day of December 2014

Janet L Carter

Notary Public for the State of Idaho

7-29-2017

Commission Expires

Rev. 08/2900

STATE OF ILLINOIS

FILED
INDEX DEPARTMENT

JAN 1 0 2011

IN THE OFFICE OF
SECRETARY OF STATE

OATH OF OFFICE

I, **PAT QUINN,** DO SOLEMNLY SWEAR THAT I WILL SUPPORT THE CONSTITUTION OF THE UNITED STATES, THE CONSTITUTION OF THE STATE OF ILLINOIS AND THE LAWS THEREOF, AND THAT I WILL FAITHFULLY DISCHARGE THE DUTIES OF **GOVERNOR OF THE STATE OF ILLINOIS** TO THE BEST OF MY ABILITY.

Pat Quinn
Pat Quinn

Subscribed and sworn to before me this 10TH day of January, 2011

Anne M. Burke
Anne M. Burke
Illinois Supreme Court Justice

131

STATE OF ILLINOIS

OATH OF OFFICE

I, **SHEILA SIMON**, DO SOLEMNLY SWEAR THAT I WILL SUPPORT THE CONSTITUTION OF THE UNITED STATES, THE CONSTITUTION OF THE STATE OF ILLINOIS AND THE LAWS THEREOF, AND THAT I WILL FAITHFULLY DISCHARGE THE DUTIES OF **LIEUTENANT GOVERNOR OF THE STATE OF ILLINOIS** TO THE BEST OF MY ABILITY.

Sheila Simon
Sheila Simon

Subscribed and sworn to before me this 10TH day of January, 2011

Mary Ann McMorrow
Mary Ann McMorrow
Justice of the Illinois Supreme Court (Retired)

132

STATE OF ILLINOIS

OATH OF OFFICE

I, **JESSE WHITE,** DO SOLEMNLY SWEAR THAT I WILL SUPPORT THE CONSTITUTION OF THE UNITED STATES, THE CONSTITUTION OF THE STATE OF ILLINOIS AND THE LAWS THEREOF, AND THAT I WILL FAITHFULLY DISCHARGE THE DUTIES OF **SECRETARY OF STATE OF ILLINOIS** TO THE BEST OF MY ABILITY.

Jesse White

Jesse White

Subscribed and sworn to before me this 10TH day of January, 2011

Joy V. Cunningham
Illinois Appellate Judge,
First District, 2nd Division

133

STATE OF ILLINOIS

I, Lisa Madigan, do solemnly swear that I will support the Constitution of the United States, and the Constitution of the State of Illinois, and that I will faithfully discharge the duties of the office of Attorney General to the best of my ability.

Subscribed and sworn to before me this 12th day of January, 2015.

The Honorable Gary S. Feinerman
Judge, United States District Court for the Northern District of Illinois

The State of Indiana

BE IT KNOWN, that pursuant to the Constitution of the State of Indiana, Article 5 and Article 15, Section 4, MIKE PENCE, hereby swears and affirms the following:

OATH OF OFFICE
GOVERNOR OF THE STATE OF INDIANA

STATE OF INDIANA
COUNTY OF MARION

I, the undersigned, do solemnly swear that I will support the Constitution of the United States and the Constitution of the State of Indiana, and that I will faithfully, impartially and diligently discharge the duties of the office of *Governor of the State of Indiana*, according to law and to the best of my ability, so help me God.

MIKE PENCE

SUBSCRIBED AND SWORN TO BEFORE ME,
THIS 14TH DAY OF JANUARY, 2013:

BRENT E. DICKSON,
CHIEF JUSTICE OF THE STATE OF INDIANA

ATTESTED BY ME,
THIS 14TH DAY OF JANUARY, 2013:

CONNIE LAWSON, INDIANA SECRETARY OF STATE

RECEIVED
IND. SECRETARY OF STATE

JAN 1 4 2013

Connie Lawson

The State of Indiana

OATH OF OFFICE
For the term beginning January 1, 2015

I do solemnly swear (or affirm) that I will faithfully discharge the duties of the office of

Secretary of State of the State of Indiana

and will support the Constitution of the United States and the Constitution of the State of Indiana to the best of my abilities, so help me God.

CONNIE LAWSON

COUNTY OF MARION)
) SS:
STATE OF INDIANA)

SUBSCRIBED AND SWORN TO BEFORE ME, this the 18th day of December, 2014, 11:?0 a.m.:

J. BRADLEY KING, L.S.
CO-DIRECTOR OF THE
INDIANA ELECTION DIVISION,
PURSUANT TO IC 33-42-4-1(11)

My Commission expires: 12-31-2014
County of Residence: Marion
FILED, in the Office of the Secretary of State, December 18, 2014, at 11:90a.m.

136

The State of Iowa refused to reply upon our request for copies of the Oath/Affirmation of their Elected Officials.

However the Elected Officials, by **Law**, are required to Sign/Autograph the Oath/Affirmation of Office.

The omittance of these documents is tantamount to "Breach of Contract" and "Obstruction of Justice".

K's

Kansas

Kentucky

Flag of the United States of the America
Title & U.S.A. Codes: Chapter 1; Section 162

Oath of Office

State of Kansas
County of **Shawnee**}SS.

I do solemnly swear, or affirm, that I will support the Constitution of the United States, and the Constitution of the State of Kansas, and will faithfully discharge the duties of the office of

Governor

So help me God.

Sam Brownback

_____
Signature

Subscribed and Sworn to, or Affirmed, before me this 10ᵗʰ day of January, A.D. 2011.

_____
Lawton R. Nuss
Chief Justice of the Supreme Court

Flag of the United States of the America
Title 4; U.S.A. Codec; Chapter 1; Section 169

Oath of Office

State of Kansas
County of **Shawnee**}SS.

I do solemnly swear, or affirm, that I will support the Constitution of the United States, and the Constitution of the State of Kansas, and will faithfully discharge the duties of the office of

Lieutenant Governor

So help me God.

Jeff Colyer

Signature

Subscribed and Sworn to, or Affirmed, before me this 12th day of January, A.D. 2015.

Lawton R. Nuss
Chief Justice of the Supreme Court

FILED

JAN 1 2 2015

KRIS W. KOBACH
SECRETARY OF STATE

Oath of Office

State of Kansas
County of **Shawnee**}SS.

I do solemnly swear, or affirm, that I will support the Constitution of the United States, and the Constitution of the State of Kansas, and will faithfully discharge the duties of the office of

Secretary of State

So help me God.

Kris W. Kobach

_____
Signature

Subscribed and Sworn to, or Affirmed, before me this 10th day of January, A.D. 2011.

_____
Lawton R. Nuss
Chief Justice of the Supreme Court

Oath of Office

State of Kansas
County of **Shawnee**}SS.

I do solemnly swear, or affirm, that I will support the Constitution of the United States, and the Constitution of the State of Kansas, and will faithfully discharge the duties of the office of

Attorney General

So help me God.

Derek Schmidt

[Signature]
Signature

Subscribed and Sworn to, or Affirmed, before me this 10th day of January, A.D. 2011.

[Signature]
Lawton R. Nuss
Chief Justice of the Supreme Court

FILED
JAN 1 0 2011
SECRETARY OF STATE

142

Flag of the United States of the America
Title: 4: U.S.A. Codex Chapter 1: Section 152

Supreme Court of Kentucky

OATH OF OFFICE
GOVERNOR OF KENTUCKY

To All To Whom These Presents Come, Greetings:

The Honorable Steven L. Beshear, having been duly elected as Governor of the Commonwealth of Kentucky for a term of four (4) years beginning December 13, 2011, whereupon the said Steven L. Beshear appeared before the Honorable J. Bill Cunningham, Justice, Supreme Court, at the Capitol in Franklin County, Kentucky at 12:01 A.M. on December 13, 2011 and took the oath as required by the Constitution of the United States, amended by Amendment XIV and Section 228 of the Kentucky Constitution.

IT IS ORDERED that the said Steven L. Beshear, having taken the oath as required by law, enter upon the discharge of his duties as Governor for the Commonwealth of Kentucky.

This the 13th day of December, 2011.

The Honorable J. Bill Cunningham
Justice
Supreme Court

Supreme Court of Kentucky

OATH OF OFFICE
GOVERNOR OF KENTUCKY

To All To Whom These Presents Come, Greetings:

The Honorable Jerry E. Abramson, having been duly elected as Lieutenant Governor of the Commonwealth of Kentucky for a term of four (4) years beginning December 13, 2011, whereupon the said Jerry E. Abramson appeared before the Honorable J. Bill Cunningham, Justice, Supreme Court, at the Capitol in Franklin County, Kentucky at 12:01 A.M. on December 13, 2011 and took the oath as required by the Constitution of the United States, amended by Amendment XIV and Section 228 of the Kentucky Constitution.

IT IS ORDERED that the said Jerry E. Abramson, having taken the oath as required by law, enter upon the discharge of his duties as Lieutenant Governor for the Commonwealth of Kentucky.

This the 13th day of December, 2011.

The Honorable J. Bill Cunningham
Justice
Supreme Court

Flag of the United States of the America
Title: a U.S.A. Codes Chapter 1: Section 152

Supreme Court of Kentucky

JUL - 7 2015

USPS

OATH OF OFFICE
KENTUCKY ATTORNEY GENERAL

To All To Whom These Presents Come, Greetings:

Honorable Jack Conway, having been elected to the Kentucky Attorney General by the citizens of the Commonwealth of Kentucky,

Whereupon, the said Honorable Jack Conway, appeared on January 2nd, 2012, in Frankfort, Kentucky before the Honorable Martin E. Johnstone, Retired Justice of the Supreme Court of Kentucky, and took the oath as required by Section 228 of the Kentucky Constitution.

Having taken the oath as required by law, IT IS ORDERED that the said Honorable Jack Conway entered upon the discharge of his duties.

This 2nd day of January, 2012.

Honorable Martin E. Johnstone
Retired Justice of the Supreme Court of Kentucky

L

Louisiana

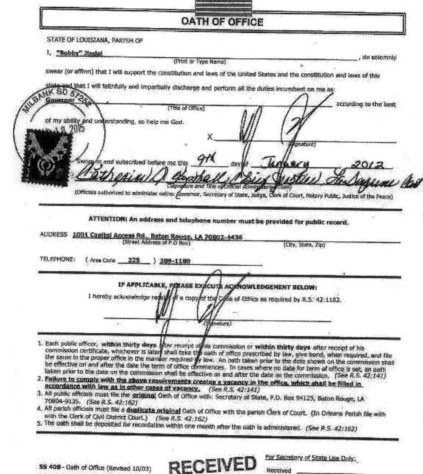

OATH OF OFFICE

STATE OF LOUISIANA, PARISH OF

I, **"Bobby" Jindal** _____ , do solemnly
                          (Print or Type Name)

swear (or affirm) that I will support the constitution and laws of the United States and the constitution and laws of this

state and that I will faithfully and impartially discharge and perform all the duties incumbent on me as

Governor _____ according to the best
                          (Title of Office)

of my ability and understanding, so help me God.

X_____
                          (Signature)

Sworn to and subscribed before me this **9th** day of **January** **2012**

_____
(Signature and Title of Official Administering Oath)

(Officials authorized to administer oaths: Governor, Secretary of State, Judge, Clerk of Court, Notary Public, Justice of the Peace)

ATTENTION: An address and telephone number must be provided for public record.

ADDRESS **1001 Capitol Access Rd., Baton Rouge, LA 70802-4436**
         (Street Address of P.O Box)   (City, State, Zip)

TELEPHONE: (Area Code **225**) **299-1180**

IF APPLICABLE, PLEASE EXECUTE ACKNOWLEDGEMENT BELOW:

I hereby acknowledge receipt of a copy of the Code of Ethics as required by R.S. 42:1182.

_____
                          (Signature)

---

1. Each public officer, **within thirty days** after receipt of his commission or **within thirty days** after receipt of his commission certificate, whichever is later, shall take the oath of office prescribed by law, give bond, when required, and file the same in the proper office in the manner required by law. An oath taken prior to the date shown on the commission shall be effective on and after the date the term of office commences. In cases where no date for term of office is set, an oath taken prior to the date on the commission shall be effective on and after the date on the commission. (See R.S. 42:141)
2. **Failure to comply with the above requirements creates a vacancy in the office, which shall be filled in accordance with law as in other cases of vacancy.** (See R.S. 42:141)
3. All public officials must file the **original** Oath of Office with: Secretary of State, P.O. Box 94125, Baton Rouge, LA 70804-9125. (See R.S. 42:162)
4. All parish officials must file a **duplicate original** Oath of Office with the parish Clerk of Court. (In Orleans Parish file with the Clerk of Civil District Court.) (See R.S. 42:162)
5. The oath shall be deposited for recordation within one month after the oath is administered. (See R.S. 42:162)

SS 408 - Oath of Office (Revised 10/03)
Prepared and Furnished by Secretary of State

RECEIVED

JAN 1 0 2012

COMMISSIONS DEPARTMENT

For Secretary of State Use Only:

Received _____

Automated _____

ID Card _____

147

Flag of the United States of America
Title 4: U.S.A. Codes: Chapter 1: Section 702

OATH OF OFFICE

STATE OF LOUISIANA, PARISH OF

I, **"Jay" Dardenne** _____ , do solemnly
                                        (Print or Type Name)

swear (or affirm) that I will support the constitution and laws of the United States and the constitution and laws of this

state and that I will faithfully and impartially discharge and perform all the duties incumbent on me as:

Lieutenant Governor _____ according to the best
                                        (Title of Office)

of my ability and understanding, so help me God.

X _____
                        (Signature)

Sworn to and subscribed before me this _____ day of _____ 2012

_____
(Signature and Title of Official Administering Oath)

(Officials authorized to administer oaths: Governor, Secretary of State, Judge, Clerk of Court, Notary Public, Justice of the Peace)

ATTENTION: An address and telephone number must be provided for public record.

ADDRESS **8855 Brookwood Dr., Baton Rouge, LA 70809-1348**
                    (Street Address or P.O Box)   (City, State, Zip)

TELEPHONE: (Area Code **225**) **663-8933**

IF APPLICABLE, PLEASE EXECUTE ACKNOWLEDGEMENT BELOW:

I hereby acknowledge receipt of a copy of the Code of Ethics as required by R.S. 42:1162.

_____
                        (Signature)

---

1. Each public officer, **within thirty days** after receipt of his commission or **within thirty days** after receipt of his commission certificate, whichever is later, shall take the oath of office prescribed by law, give bond, when required, and file the same in the proper office in the manner required by law. An oath taken prior to the date shown on the commission shall be effective on and after the date the term of office commences. In cases where no date for term of office is set, an oath taken prior to the date on the commission shall be effective on and after the date on the commission. *(See R.S. 42:141)*
2. **Failure to comply with the above requirements creates a vacancy in the office, which shall be filled in accordance with law as in other cases of vacancy.** *(See R.S. 42:141)*
3. All public officials must file the **original** Oath of Office with: Secretary of State, P.O. Box 94125, Baton Rouge, LA 70804-9125. *(See R.S. 42:162)*
4. All parish officials must file a **duplicate original** Oath of Office with the parish Clerk of Court. (In Orleans Parish file with with the Clerk of Civil District Court.) *(See R.S. 42:162)*
5. The oath shall be deposited for recordation within one month after the oath is administered. *(See R.S. 42:162)*

For Secretary of State Use Only:

SS 408 - Oath of Office (Revised 10/03)   Received _____
Prepared and Furnished by Secretary of State

RECEIVED   Automated _____

JAN 1 0 2012   ID Card _____

COMMISSIONS DEPARTMENT

OATH OF OFFICE

STATE OF LOUISIANA, PARISH OF EAST BATON ROUGE

Flag of the United States of the America
Title X: U.S.A. Codes: Colorian; ti Sections; 152

I, **Tom Schedler** _____ , do solemnly
_____
(Print or Type Name)

swear (or affirm) that I will support the constitution and laws of the United States and the constitution and laws of this

state and that I will faithfully and impartially discharge and perform all the duties incumbent on me as:

Secretary of State _____ according to the best
_____
(Title of Office)

of my ability and understanding, so help me God.

X _____
(Signature)

Sworn to and subscribed before me this **22nd** day of **November**, **2010**

_____
(Signature and Title of Official Administering Oath)   Notary Public
(Officials authorized to administer oaths: Governor, Secretary of State, Judge, Clerk of Court, Notary Public, Justice of the Peace)
John J. Portemay. Bar Roll 4543

ATTENTION: An address and telephone number must be provided for public record.

ADDRESS **7211 Brookwood Dr., Mandeville, LA 70471** _____
(Street Address of P.O Box)   (City, State, Zip)

TELEPHONE: (Area Code **225**) **922-2880** _____

IF APPLICABLE, PLEASE EXECUTE ACKNOWLEDGEMENT BELOW:

I hereby acknowledge receipt of a copy of the Code of Ethics as required by R.S. 42:1162.

_____
(Signature)

1. Each public officer, **within thirty days** after receipt of his commission or **within thirty days** after receipt of his commission certificate, whichever is later, shall take the oath of office prescribed by law, give bond, when required, and file the same in the proper office in the manner required by law. An oath taken prior to the date shown on the commission shall be effective on and after the date the term of office commences. In cases where no date for term of office is set, an oath taken prior to the date on the commission shall be effective on and after the date on the commission. (See R.S. 42:141)
2. **Failure to comply with the above requirements creates a vacancy in the office, which shall be filled in accordance with law as in other cases of vacancy.** (See R.S. 42:141)
3. All public officials must file the **original** Oath of Office with: Secretary of State, P.O. Box 94125, Baton Rouge, LA 70804-9125. (See R.S. 42:162)
4. All parish officials must file a **duplicate original** Oath of Office with the parish Clerk of Court. (In Orleans Parish file with with the Clerk of Civil District Court.) (See R.S. 42:162)
5. The oath shall be deposited for recordation within one month after the oath is administered. (See R.S. 42:162)

SS 408 - Oath of Office (Revised 10/03)
Prepared and Furnished by Secretary of State

RECEIVED
COMMISSIONS DEPT.

NOV 22 2010

SECRETARY OF STATE

For Secretary of State Use Only:

Received _____

Automated _____

ID Card _____

149

OATH OF OFFICE

STATE OF LOUISIANA, PARISH OF _____

I, **James D. "Buddy" Caldwell** _____, do solemnly

(Print or Type Name)

swear (or affirm) that I will support the constitution and laws of the United States and the constitution and laws of this

state and that I will faithfully and impartially discharge and perform all the duties incumbent on me as:

Attorney General _____ according to the best

(Title of Office)

of my ability and understanding, so help me God.

(Signature)

Sworn to and subscribed before me this _7th_ day of _January_ _2012_

(Signature and Title of Officer Administering Oath) _Second Circuit Court of App_

(Officials authorized to administer oaths: Governor, Secretary of State, Judge, Clerk of Court, Notary Public, Justice of the Peace)

ATTENTION: An address and telephone number must be provided for public record.

ADDRESS **96 Marianna, Tallulah, LA 71282-5580**

(Street Address of P.O Box)   (City, State, Zip)

TELEPHONE: (Area Code _318_) _574-4771_

IF APPLICABLE, PLEASE EXECUTE ACKNOWLEDGEMENT BELOW:

I hereby acknowledge receipt of a copy of the Code of Ethics as required by R.S. 42:1162.

(Signature)

1. Each public officer, **within thirty days** after receipt of his commission or **within thirty days** after receipt of his commission certificate, whichever is later, shall take the oath of office prescribed by law, give bond, when required, and file the same in the proper office in the manner required by law. An oath taken prior to the date shown on the commission shall be effective on and after the date the term of office commences. In cases where no date for term of office is set, an oath taken prior to the date on the commission shall be effective on and after the date on the commission. (See R.S. 42:141)
2. **Failure to comply with the above requirements creates a vacancy in the office, which shall be filled in accordance with law as in other cases of vacancy.** (See R.S. 42:141)
3. All public officials must file the **original** Oath of Office with: Secretary of State, P.O. Box 94125, Baton Rouge, LA 70804-9125. (See R.S. 42:162)
4. All parish officials must file a **duplicate original** Oath of Office with the parish Clerk of Court. (In Orleans Parish file with with the Clerk of Civil District Court.) (See R.S. 42:162)
5. The oath shall be deposited for recordation within one month after the oath is administered. (See R.S. 42:162)

SS 408 - Oath of Office (Revised 10/03)

Prepared and Furnished by Secretary of State

RECEIVED

JAN 1 0 2012

COMMISSIONS DEPARTMENT

For Secretary of State Use Only:

Received _____

Automated _____

ID Card _____

M's

Maine

Maryland

Massachusetts

Michigan

Minnesota

Mississippi

Missouri

Montana

Certificate of Qualification, Governor

State of Maine

I,   **Paul R. LePage**
do swear, that I will support the Constitution of the United States, and of this State, so long as I shall continue a citizen thereof.

So Help Me God.

_____
Paul R. LePage, Governor

I,   **Paul R. LePage**
do swear, that I will faithfully discharge, to the best of my abilities, the duties incumbent on me as *Governor* of the State of Maine, according to the Constitution and Laws of the State.

So Help Me God.

_____
Paul R. LePage, Governor

≈ ≈ ≈ ≈ ≈ ≈ ≈ ≈ ≈

At Augusta, on the seventh day of January in the year Two Thousand and Fifteen, personally appeared *Paul R. LePage* of *Augusta* and took and subscribed the oaths prescribed by the Constitution of this State, to qualify him to discharge and execute the duties of the office of Governor of the State of Maine.

_____
Michael D. Thibodeau, President of the Senate

This certificate to be filed with the Secretary of State of Maine.

Certificate of Qualification, Attorney General

State of Maine

I, **Janet T. Mills**

do swear, that I will support the Constitution of the United States, and of this State, so long as I shall continue a citizen thereof.

So Help Me God.

Janet T. Mills, *Attorney General*

I, **Janet T. Mills**

*do swear, that I will faithfully discharge, to the best of my abilities, the duties incumbent on me as **Attorney General** of the State of Maine, according to the Constitution and Laws of the State.*

So Help Me God.

Janet T. Mills, *Attorney General*

*At Augusta, on the eighth day of January in the year Two Thousand and Fifteen, personally appeared **Janet T. Mills of Farmington** and took and subscribed the oaths prescribed by the Constitution of this State, to qualify her to discharge and execute the duties of the office of **Attorney General** of the State of Maine.*

Paul R. LePage, *Governor*

This certificate to be filed with the Secretary of State of Maine.

153

State of Maine

I,   **Matthew Dunlap**

do swear, that I will support the Constitution of the United States, and of this State, so long as I shall continue a citizen thereof.

So Help Me God.

Matthew Dunlap, Secretary of State

I,   **Matthew Dunlap**

do swear, that I will faithfully discharge, to the best of my abilities, the duties incumbent on me as **Secretary of State** *of the State of Maine, according to the Constitution and Laws of the State.*

So Help Me God.

Matthew Dunlap, Secretary of State

At Augusta, on the eighth day of January in the year Two Thousand and Fifteen, personally appeared **Matthew Dunlap of Old Town** *and took and subscribed the oaths prescribed by the Constitution of this State, to qualify him to discharge and execute the duties of the office of* **Secretary of State** *of the State of Maine.*

Paul R. LePage, Governor

This certificate to be filed with the Secretary of State of Maine.

Certificate of Qualification, State Treasurer

State of Maine

Teresea M. Hayes

I,

do swear, that I will support the Constitution of the United States, and of this State, so long as I shall continue a citizen thereof.

So Help Me God.

_____
Teresea M. Hayes, State Treasurer

I,   **Teresea M. Hayes**

do swear, that I will faithfully discharge, to the best of my abilities, the duties incumbent on me as **State Treasurer** of the State of Maine, according to the Constitution and Laws of the State.

So Help Me God.

_____
Teresea M. Hayes, State Treasurer

At Augusta, on the eighth day of January in the year Two Thousand and Fifteen, personally appeared **Teresea M. Hayes of Buckfield** and took and subscribed the oaths prescribed by the Constitution of this State, to qualify her to discharge and execute the duties of the office of **State Treasurer** of the State of Maine.

_____
Paul R. LePage, Governor

This certificate to be filed with the Secretary of State of Maine

The State of Maryland refused to reply upon our request for copies of the Oath/Affirmation of their Elected Officials.

However the Elected Officials, by **Law**, are required to Sign/Autograph the Oath/Affirmation of Office.

The omittance of these documents is tantamount to "Breach of Contract" and "Obstruction of Justice".

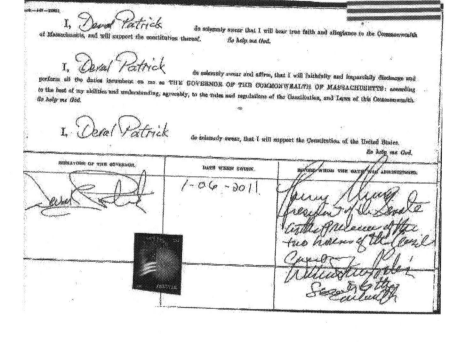

I, Deval Patrick of Massachusetts, and will support the constitution thereof. do solemnly swear that I will bear true faith and allegiance to the Commonwealth So help me God.

I, Deval Patrick do solemnly swear and affirm, that I will faithfully and impartially discharge and perform all the duties incumbent on me as THE GOVERNOR OF THE COMMONWEALTH OF MASSACHUSETTS : according to the best of my abilities and understanding, agreeably, to the rules and regulations of the Constitution, and Laws of this Commonwealth. So help me God.

I, Deval Patrick do solemnly swear, that I will support the Constitution of the United States. So help me God.

SIGNATURE OF THE GOVERNOR.	DATE WHEN SWORN.	BEFORE WHOM THE OATH WAS ADMINISTERED.
	1-06-2011	

I book — 4-87 — 9.1912

I, KARYN POLITO do solemnly swear that I will bear true faith and allegiance to the Commonwealth of Massachusetts, and will support the constitution thereof. So help me God.

I, _____ do solemnly swear and affirm, that I will faithfully and impartially discharge and perform all the duties incumbent on me as THE LIEUTENANT-GOVERNOR OF THE COMMONWEALTH OF MASSACHU-SETTS; according to the best of my abilities and understanding, agreeably, to the rules and regulations of the Constitution, and Laws of this Commonwealth. So help me God.

I, _____ do solemnly swear, that I will support the Constitution of the United States. So help me God.

SIGNATURE OF THE LIEUT.-GOVERNOR.	DATE WHEN SWORN.	BEFORE WHOM THE OATH WAS ADMINISTERED.
	1/9/15	

158

The Commonwealth of Massachusetts

William Francis Galvin
Secretary of the Commonwealth - Commissions Section
One Ashburton Place - Room 1719, Boston, Massachusetts 02108

Form O

I (name) do solemnly swear that I will bear true faith and allegiance to the Commonwealth of Massachusetts, and will support the constitution thereof - So help me God.

I (name) do solemnly swear and affirm, that I will faithfully and impartially discharge and perform all the duties incumbent on me as (TITLE) - according to the best of my abilities and understanding, agreeably, to the rules and regulations of the Constitution, and the laws of this Commonwealth - So help me God.

I (name) do solemnly swear that I will support the Constitution of the United States.

Signature _____ William Francis Galvin
(please sign)   (please print or type name)

Title of Office: Secretary of the Commonwealth

Residence: ████████████████████

Date of Appointment: January 19, 2011

Date of Qualification: January 19, 2011

Personally appeared the above signed who took and subscribed the Oaths prescribed by the Constitution of this Commonwealth and a law of the United States to qualify him to discharge the duties of the office to which he is appointed by Commission.

Commissioners to Qualify Public Officers

Before us: _____ Deval L. Patrick
(please sign)   (please print or type name)

_____ _____
(please sign)   (please print or type name)

COMMISSIONERS TO QUALIFY - PLEASE NOTE
Appointee should receive a copy of this certificate (Form O) and the original should be forwarded to the Office of the Secretary of the Commonwealth, Room 1719 - Commissions Section, McCormack Building, One Ashburton Place, Boston, MA 02108

THE COMMONWEALTH OF MASSACHUSETTS

I (name) do solemnly swear that I will bear true faith and allegiance to the Commonwealth of Massachusetts, and will support the constitution thereof - So help me God

I (name) do solemnly swear and affirm, that I will faithfully and impartially discharge and perform all the duties incumbent on me as (TITLE)- according to the best of my abilities and understanding, agreeably, to the rules and regulations of the Constitution, and the laws of this Commonwealth - So help me God.

I (name) do solemnly swear that I will support the Constitution of the United States.

Signature

Title of Office

Martha Coakley, Attorney General

Residence

Date of Appointment

January 19, 2011

Date of Qualification

January 19, 2011

Personally appeared the above signed who took and subscribed the Oaths prescribed by the Constitution of this Commonwealth and a law of the United States to qualify him to discharge the duties of the office to which he is appointed by Commission.

Commissioners to Qualify Public Officers

Before us:

Edward Bedrosian, Jr., First Assistant Attorney General

Sheila M. Calkins, Deputy 1st Assistant Attorney General/Chief of Staff

* *COMMISSIONERS TO QUALIFY* * *PLEASE NOTE* * *

Appointee should receive a copy of this certificate (Form 0) and the original should be forwarded to the:

Office of the Secretary of the Commonwealth, Room 1719 - Commissions Section, McCormack Building, One Ashburton Place, Boston, MA 02108

Form 0

THE COMMONWEALTH OF MASSACHUSETTS

I (name) do solemnly swear that I will bear true faith and allegiance to the Commonwealth of Massachusetts, and will support the constitution thereof - So help me God

I (name) do solemnly swear and affirm, that I will faithfully and impartially discharge and perform all the duties incumbent on me as (TITLE)- according to the best of my abilities and understanding, agreeably, to the rules and regulations of the Constitution, and the laws of this Commonwealth - So help me God.

I (name) do solemnly swear that I will support the Constitution of the United States.

Signature *Martha Coakley*

Title of Office

Martha Coakley, Attorney General

Residence

Date of Appointment

January 19, 2011

Date of Qualification

January 19, 2011

Personally appeared the above signed who took and subscribed the Oaths prescribed by the Constitution of this Commonwealth and a law of the United States to qualify him to discharge the duties of the office to which he is appointed by Commission.

Commissioners to Qualify Public Officers

Before us:

Edward Bedrosian, Jr., First Assistant Attorney General

Sheila M. Calkins, Deputy 1st Assistant Attorney General/Chief of Staff

* *"COMMISSIONERS TO QUALIFY* * *" PLEASE NOTE* * *

Appointee should receive a copy of this certificate (Form 0) and the original should be forwarded to the:

Office of the Secretary of the Commonwealth, Room 1719 - Commissions Section, McCormack Building, One Ashburton Place, Boston, MA 02108

OATH OF OFFICE

STATE OF MICHIGAN }
County of _ＩＮＧＨＡＭ_ } SS.

I do solemnly swear that I will support the Constitution of the United States and the

Constitution of this State, and that I will faithfully discharge the duties of the office of

GOVERNOR

according to the best of my ability.

Signature

RICHARD D. SNYDER
Name Printed or Typed

Sworn to and subscribed before me this 30ᵗʰ *day of* DECEMBER, 2010

20

Signature

NOTARY PUBLIC
Title

ALLISON SCOTT
Name Printed or Typed

Name of Notary: ALLISON SCOTT
County: JACKSON
Acting in: INGHAM
Commission
Expires: 10-27-12

* This information is requested if Oath of Office is taken before someone other than a notary public.

**When filing with the Secretary of State, original signatures are required.

Form 32-5/99-5M

162

OATH OF OFFICE

STATE OF MICHIGAN

County of **Ingham** } ss.

I do solemnly swear that I will support the Constitution of the United States and the

Constitution of this State, and that I will faithfully discharge the duties of the office of

Lt. Governor

according to the best of my ability.

_____ **

Signature

Brian N. Calley

Name Printed or Typed

Sworn to and subscribed before me this **15th** *day of* **December**, 20 **14**

_____ **

Signature

_____ *

Title

_____ *

Name Printed or Typed

Notary Public, State of Michigan, County of **Clinton**

My Commission Expires **12-29-2016**

Acting in the County of **Ingham**

CHERYL J. ARWOOD
NOTARY PUBLIC-STATE OF MICHIGAN
COUNTY OF CLINTON
My Commission Expires Dec. 29, 2016

*This information is requested if Oath of Office is taken before someone other than a notary public

**When filing with the Secretary of State, original signatures are required

163

OATH OF OFFICE

STATE OF MICHIGAN
County of **Ingham** } SS.

I do solemnly swear that I will support the Constitution of the United States and the

Constitution of this State, and that I will faithfully discharge the duties of the office of

Secretary of State

according to the best of my ability.

Signature **

Ruth A. Johnson
Name Printed or Typed

Sworn to and subscribed before me this **1st** day of **January** 20 **11**

Signature **

Title *

Name Printed or Typed *

Notary Public, State of Michigan, County of **Clinton**

My Commission Expires **12-29-2016**

Acting in the County of **Ingham**

*This information is required if Oath of Office is taken before someone other than a notary public

**When filing with the Secretary of State, original signatures are required

OATH OF OFFICE

STATE OF MICHIGAN }
County of _Ingham_ } SS.

I do solemnly swear that I will support the Constitution of the United States and the

Constitution of this State, and that I will faithfully discharge the duties of the office of

Attorney General

according to the best of my ability.

Bill Schuette
<small>Signature</small> **

BILL SCHUETTE
<small>Name Printed or Typed</small>

Sworn to and subscribed before me this 1st *day of* January
2011

Richard A. Bandstra
<small>Signature</small> **

JUDGE, MICHIGAN COURT OF APPEALS
<small>Title</small>

RICHARD A. BANDSTRA
<small>Name Printed or Typed</small>

Name of Notary:
County:
Commission
Expires:

* This information is requested if Oath of Office is taken before
someone other than a notary public.

** When filing with the Secretary of State, original signatures are required.

Form 33-5199-5M

State of Minnesota
Oath of Office for Governor

Mark Dayton

*I, Mark Dayton, do solemnly swear that
I will support the Constitution of the United States and the
Constitution of the State of Minnesota; and that
I will discharge faithfully the duties of the
Office of Governor
to the best of my judgment and ability, so help me God.*

I certify that I am authorized to execute this oath, and I further certify that I understand that by signing this oath, I am subject to the penalties of perjury as set forth in *Minnesota Statutes* 609.48 as if I had signed this oath before a notary public.

January 3, 2011

_____
Governor

_____
Judge

110145 Secretary of State

State of Minnesota
Oath of Office for Attorney General

 Lori Swanson

I, Lori Swanson, do solemnly swear that I will support the Constitution of the United States and the Constitution of the State of Minnesota, and that I will discharge faithfully the duties of the Office of Attorney General to the best of my judgment and ability, so help me God.

I certify that I am authorized to execute this oath, and I further certify that I understand that by signing this oath, I am subject to the penalties of perjury as set forth in *Minnesota Statutes 609.48* as if I had signed this oath before a notary public.

January 3, 2011

_____
Attorney General

_____
Judge

1101457 Secretary of State

167

The State of Mississippi refused to reply upon our request for copies of the Oath/Affirmation of their Elected Officials.

However the Elected Officials, by **Law**, are required to Sign/Autograph the Oath/Affirmation of Office.

The omittance of these documents is tantamount to "Breach of Contract" and "Obstruction of Justice".

JEREMIAH W. (JAY) NIXON
GOVERNOR

GOVERNOR OF MISSOURI
JEFFERSON CITY
65102

P.O. Box 720
(573) 751-3222

Missouri Gov. Jeremiah Willson (Jay) Nixon

Oath of Office, administered by Circuit Judge Rex M. Burlison of the 22nd Judicial Circuit to Gov. Nixon upon the inauguration of his second term as Missouri's 55th Governor

Noon CST, Monday, January 14, 2013

CIRCUIT JUDGE REX BURLISON: Governor, would you please raise your right hand and repeat after me. I, Jeremiah Willson Nixon...

GOV. NIXON: I, Jeremiah Willson Nixon...

JUDGE BURLISON: Do solemnly swear...

GOV. NIXON: Do solemnly swear...

JUDGE BURLISON: To support the Constitution of the United States...

GOV. NIXON: To support the Constitution of the United States...

JUDGE BURLISON: And the Constitution of the State of Missouri...

GOV. NIXON: And the Constitution of Missouri...

JUDGE BURLISON: And to demean myself faithfully ...

GOV. NIXON: And to demean myself faithfully ...

JUDGE BURLISON: In the Office of...

GOV. NIXON: In the Office of...

JUDGE BURLISON: Governor of the State of Missouri...

GOV. NIXON: Governor of the State of Missouri...

JUDGE BURLISON: So help me God.

GOV. NIXON: So help me God.

www.governor.mo.gov

ATTORNEY GENERAL OF MISSOURI

JEFFERSON CITY

65102

CHRIS KOSTER
ATTORNEY GENERAL

P.O. Box 899
(573) 751-0321

Missouri Attorney General Chris Koster

Oath of Office, administered by The Honorable Judge Mary Russell to Attorney General Koster upon the inauguration of his second term as Missouri's 41st Attorney General

Noon CST, Monday, January 14, 2013

The Honorable Judge Mary Russell: Attorney General, would you please raise your right hand and repeat after me. I, Christopher A Koster...

ATTORNEY GENERAL KOSTER: I, Christopher A Koster

JUDGE RUSSELL: Do solemnly swear...

ATTORNEY GENERAL KOSTER: Do solemnly swear

JUDGE RUSSELL: That I will support the Constitution

ATTORNEY GENERAL KOSTER: That I will support the Constitution

JUDGE RUSSELL: of the United States...

ATTORNEY GENERAL KOSTER: of the United States...

JUDGE RUSSELL: And of the State of Missouri...

ATTORNEY GENERAL KOSTER: And of the State of Missouri...

JUDGE RUSSELL: And I will faithfully demean myself....

ATTORNEY GENERAL KOSTER: And I will faithfully demean myself...

JUDGE RUSSELL: In the Office of...

ATTORNEY GENERAL KOSTER: In the Office of...

JUDGE RUSSELL: Attorney General of the State of Missouri

ATTORNEY GENERAL KOSTER: Attorney General of the State of Missouri

JUDGE RUSSELL: So help me God.

ATTORNEY GENERAL KOSTER: So help me God.

OATH OF OFFICE

State of Montana)
) ss
County of Lewis & Clark)

I, **Steve Bullock,** do solemnly swear (or affirm) that I will support, protect and defend the Constitution of the United States, and the Constitution of the state of Montana, and that I will discharge the duties of my office (**Governor**) with fidelity (so help me God).

In addition, in accordance with § 2-16-114, Montana Code Annotated, I certify that my signature below is my true and correct manual signature, and is in the exact form in which it will appear in facsimile upon any document which I may be required or permitted by law to sign.

Steve Bullock

Sworn to and subscribed before me this 7th day of January, A.D. 2013.

(SEAL)

Mike McGrath
Chief Justice
Montana Supreme Court

RESERVED FOR SECRETARY OF STATE USE ONLY
Filed on January 7th 2013 under oath number 1-2013 for the
Secretary of State, by Shannon H. Stevens, Legislative Specialist. 8351

171

OATH OF OFFICE

State of Montana)
) ss
County of Lewis & Clark .)

I, **Tim Fox**, do solemnly swear (or affirm) that I will support, protect and defend the Constitution of the United States, and the Constitution of the state of Montana, and that I will discharge the duties of my office (**Attorney General**) with fidelity (so help me God).

In addition, in accordance with § 2-16-114, Montana Code Annotated, I certify that my signature below is my true and correct manual signature, and is in the exact form in which it will appear in facsimile upon any document which I may be required or permitted by law to sign.

Tim Fox

Sworn to and subscribed before me this 7th day of January, A.D. 2013.

(SEAL)

Mike McGrath
Chief Justice
Montana Supreme Court

OATH OF OFFICE

State of Montana   )
) ss
County of Lewis & Clark .)

I, **Linda McCulloch**, do solemnly swear (or affirm) that I will support, protect and defend the Constitution of the United States, and the Constitution of the state of Montana, and that I will discharge the duties of my office (**Secretary of State**) with fidelity (so help me God).

In addition, in accordance with § 2-16-114, Montana Code Annotated, I certify that my signature below is my true and correct manual signature, and is in the exact form in which it will appear in facsimile upon any document which I may be required or permitted by law to sign.

Linda McCulloch

Sworn to and subscribed before me this 7th day of January, A.D. 2013.

(SEAL)

Mike McGrath
Chief Justice
Montana Supreme Court

IN THE NAME AND BY THE AUTHORITY OF THE

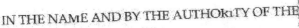

Oath of Office

State of Montana   )
                                    : ss
County of Anaconda-Deer Lodge   )

I, ANGELA MCLEAN, do solemnly swear (or affirm) that I will support, protect and defend the Constitution of the United States, and the Constitution of the State of Montana, and that I will discharge the duties of my office with fidelity (so help me God).

In addition, in accordance with § 2-16-114, Montana Code Annotated, I certify that my signature below is my true and correct manual signature, and is in the exact form in which it will appear in facsimile upon any document which I may be required or permitted by law to sign.

_____
ANGELA MCLEAN

Sworn to and subscribed before me this _10_ day of February, A.D. 2014

_____
HONORABLE RAY J. DAYTON
Third Judicial District

LYDIA JANOSKO
NOTARY PUBLIC for the
STATE OF MONTANA
Residing in Anaconda, Montana
My Commission Expires
January 22, 2016

_____
Notary Public for the State of Montana

Lydia Janosko
Printed Name of Notary Public
Residing at Anaconda
My Commission Expires Jan. 22, 2016

SECRETARY OF STATE USE ONLY: Filed this 11th day of February, 2014
under oath Statewide   by Shannon H. Stevens, Legislative Specialist.

174

N's

Nebraska

Nevada

New Hampshire

New Jersey

New Mexico

New York

North Carolina

North Dakota

STATE OF NEBRASKA
OATH OF OFFICE

STATE OF NEBRASKA)
)ss.
County of Lancaster)

"I, **Pete Ricketts,** do solemnly swear (or affirm) that I will support the
Constitution of the United States, and the Constitution of the State of
Nebraska, and will faithfully discharge the duties of **Governor,** according to
the best of my ability, and that at the election at which I was chosen to fill said
office, I have not improperly influenced in any way the vote of any elector, and
have not accepted, nor will I accept or receive, directly or indirectly, any money
or other valuable thing from any corporation, company or person, or any
promise of office, for any official act or influence (for any vote may give or
withhold on any bill, resolution, or appropriation)."*

Pete Ricketts

Subscribed in my presence and sworn to before
me this **8th** day of *January, 2015.*

John A. Gale
Secretary of State

*Constitution of the State of Nebraska, Article XV, Section One.
For Executive, Judicial Officers and Members of the Legislature.

176

STATE OF NEBRASKA
OATH OF OFFICE

STATE OF NEBRASKA   }
         }ss.
County of Lancaster   }

"I, **Mike Foley,** do solemnly swear (or affirm) that I will support the Constitution of the United States, and the Constitution of the State of Nebraska, and will faithfully discharge the duties of **Lieutenant Governor,** according to the best of my ability, and that at the election at which I was chosen to fill said office, I have not improperly influenced in any way the vote of any elector, and have not accepted, nor will I accept or receive, directly or indirectly, any money or other valuable thing from any corporation, company or person, or any promise of office, for any official act or influence (for any vote may give or withhold on any bill, resolution, or appropriation)."*

_____
Mike Foley

Subscribed in my presence and sworn to before me this **8th** day of **January, 2015.**

_____
John A. Gale
Secretary of State

*Constitution of the State of Nebraska, Article XV, Section One.
For Executive, Judicial Officers and Members of the Legislature.

STATE OF NEBRASKA
OATH OF OFFICE

STATE OF NEBRASKA   )
)ss.
County of Lancaster   )

"I, **John A. Gale,** do solemnly swear (or affirm) that I will support the Constitution of the United States, and the Constitution of the State of Nebraska, and will faithfully discharge the duties of **Secretary of State,** according to the best of my ability, and that at the election at which I was chosen to fill said office, I have not improperly influenced in any way the vote of any elector, and have not accepted, nor will I accept or receive, directly or indirectly, any money or other valuable thing from any corporation, company or person, or any promise of office, for any official act or influence (for any vote may give or withhold on any bill, resolution, or appropriation)."*

_____
John Gale

Subscribed in my presence and sworn to before me this **8th** day of *January, 2015*.

_____
Notary or Witness Authorized
to Administer Oath

GENERAL NOTARY - State of Nebraska
JONI L. SAILORS
My Comm. Exp. December 23, 2015

*Constitution of the State of Nebraska, Article XV, Section One.
For Executive, Judicial Officers and Members of the Legislature.

STATE OF NEBRASKA
OATH OF OFFICE

STATE OF NEBRASKA)
))ss.
County of Lancaster)

*I, **Doug Peterson**, do solemnly swear (or affirm) that I will support the Constitution of the United States, and the Constitution of the State of Nebraska, and will faithfully discharge the duties of **Attorney General,** according to the best of my ability, and that at the election at which I was chosen to fill said office, I have not improperly influenced in any way the vote of any elector, and have not accepted, nor will I accept or receive, directly or indirectly, any money or other valuable thing from any corporation, company or person, or any promise of office, for any official act or influence (for any vote may give or withhold on any bill, resolution, or appropriation).**

Doug Peterson

Subscribed in my presence and sworn to before me this **8th** day of **January, 2015.**

John A. Gale
Secretary of State

*Constitution of the State of Nebraska, Article XV, Section One.
For Executive, Judicial Officers and Members of the Legislature.

179

STATE OF NEVADA

Executive Department

CERTIFICATE OF ELECTION

This is to certify that at a general election held in the State of Nevada on Tuesday, the second day of November, two thousand ten

BRIAN E. SANDOVAL

was duly elected to the office of Governor of the State of Nevada, for the term of four years from and including the first Monday in January, two thousand eleven;

Now, Therefore, I Jim Gibbons, Governor of the State of Nevada, by the authority vested in me by the Constitution and laws thereof, do hereby

COMMISSION

him, the said BRIAN E. SANDOVAL as Governor of the State of Nevada, and authorize him to discharge the duties of said office according to law, and to hold and enjoy the same, together with all powers, privileges and emoluments thereunto appertaining.

In Testimony Thereof, I have hereunto set my hand and caused the Great Seal of the State of Nevada to be affixed at the State Capitol at Carson City, Nevada on this 14th day of December, two thousand ten.

Governor of the State of Nevada

Secretary of State of Nevada

I, BRIAN E. SANDOVAL, do solemnly swear that I will support, protect and defend the constitution and government of the United States, and the constitution and government of the State of Nevada, against all enemies, whether domestic or foreign, and that I will bear true faith, allegiance and loyalty to the same, any ordinance, resolution or law of any state notwithstanding, and that I will well and faithfully perform all the duties of the office of Governor of the State of Nevada, on which I am about to enter; so help me God.

State of Nevada

County of Carson

Subscribed and Sworn to before me this 3rd day of January A.D., two thousand eleven.

Chief Justice Nevada Supreme Court

180

CERTIFICATE OF ELECTION

This is to certify that at a general election held in the State of Nevada on Tuesday, the second day of November, two thousand ten

BRIAN K. KROLICKI

was duly elected to the office of Lieutenant Governor of the State of Nevada, for the term of four years from and including the first Monday in January, two thousand eleven:

Now, Therefore, I Jim Gibbons, Governor of the State of Nevada, by the authority vested in me by the Constitution and laws thereof, do hereby

COMMISSION

him, the said BRIAN K. KROLICKI as Lieutenant Governor of the State of Nevada, and authorize him to discharge the duties of said office according to law, and to hold and enjoy the same together with all powers, privileges and emoluments thereunto appertaining.

In Testimony Thereof, I have hereunto set my hand and caused the Great Seal of the State of Nevada to be affixed at the State Capitol at Carson City, Nevada on this 14th day of December, two thousand ten.

Governor of the State of Nevada

Secretary of State of Nevada

I, BRIAN K. KROLICKI, do solemnly swear that I will support, protect and defend the constitution and government of the United States, and the constitution and government of the State of Nevada, against all enemies, whether domestic or foreign, and that I will bear true faith, allegiance and loyalty to the same, any ordinance, resolution or law of any state notwithstanding, and that I will well and faithfully perform all the duties of the office of Lieutenant Governor of the State of Nevada, on which I am about to enter; so help me God.

State of Nevada

County of Carson

Subscribed and Sworn to before me this 3d day of Jan A.D., two thousand eleven.

181

STATE OF NEVADA

Executive Department

CERTIFICATE OF ELECTION

This is to certify that at a general election held in the State of Nevada on Tuesday, the second day of November, two thousand ten

ROSS MILLER

was duly elected to the office of Secretary of State of the State of Nevada, for the term of four years from and including the first Monday in January, two thousand eleven;

Now, Therefore, I Jim Gibbons, Governor of the State of Nevada, by the authority vested in me by the Constitution and laws thereof, do hereby

COMMISSION

him, the said ROSS MILLER as Secretary of State of the State of Nevada, and authorize him to discharge the duties of said office according to law, and to hold and enjoy the same together with all powers, privileges and emoluments thereunto appertaining.

In Testimony Thereof, I have hereunto set my hand and caused the Great Seal of the State of Nevada to be affixed at the State Capitol at Carson City, Nevada on this 14th day of December, two thousand ten

_____
Governor of the State of Nevada

_____
Secretary of State of Nevada

I, ROSS MILLER, do solemnly swear that I will support, protect and defend the constitution and government of the United States, and the constitution and government of the State of Nevada, against all enemies, whether domestic or foreign, and that I will bear true faith, allegiance and loyalty to the same, any ordinance, resolution or law of any state notwithstanding, and that I will well and faithfully perform all the duties of the office of Secretary of State of the State of Nevada, on which I am about to enter; so help me God.

_____

State of Nevada

County of Carson

Subscribed and Sworn to before me this 3 RD day of January A.D., two thousand eleven.

_____

Chief Justice Nevada Supreme Court

STATE OF NEVADA
Executive Department

CERTIFICATE OF ELECTION

This is to certify that at a general election held in the State of Nevada on Tuesday, the second day of November, two thousand ten

CATHERINE CORTEZ MASTO

was duly elected to the office of Attorney General of the State of Nevada, for the term of four years from and including the first Monday in January, two thousand eleven;

Now, Therefore, I Jim Gibbons, Governor of the State of Nevada, by the authority vested in me by the Constitution and laws thereof, do hereby

COMMISSION

her, the said CATHERINE CORTEZ MASTO as Attorney General of the State of Nevada, and authorize her to discharge the duties of said office according to law, and to hold and enjoy the same together with all powers, privileges and emoluments thereunto appertaining.

In Testimony Thereof, I have hereunto set my hand and caused the Great Seal of the State of Nevada to be affixed at the State Capitol at Carson City, Nevada on this 14th day of December, two thousand ten.

Governor of the State of Nevada

Secretary of State of Nevada

I, CATHERINE CORTEZ MASTO, do solemnly swear that I will support, protect and defend the constitution and government of the United States, and the constitution and government of the State of Nevada, against all enemies, whether domestic or foreign, and that I will bear true faith, allegiance and loyalty to the same, any ordinance, resolution or law of any state notwithstanding, and that I will seek and faithfully perform all the duties of the office of Attorney General of the State of Nevada on which I am about to enter; so help me God.

State of Nevada

County of Carson

Subscribed and Sworn to before me this _3rd_ day _January_ A.D., two thousand eleven.

Chief Clerk Nevada Supreme Court

183

The State of New Hampshire refused to reply upon our request for copies of the Oath/Affirmation of their Elected Officials.

However the Elected Officials, by **Law**, are required to Sign/Autograph the Oath/Affirmation of Office.

The omittance of these documents is tantamount to "Breach of Contract" and "Obstruction of Justice".

GOVERNOR OF THE STATE OF NEW JERSEY

STATE OF NEW JERSEY)
)ss.
COUNTY OF MERCER)

    I, CHRIS CHRISTIE, elected Governor of the State of New Jersey, do solemnly promise and swear that I will support the Constitution of the United States and the Constitution of the State of New Jersey, and that I will bear true faith and allegiance to the same and to the Governments established in the United States and in this State, under the authority of the people; and that I will diligently, faithfully, impartially, justly and to the best of my knowledge and ability, execute the said office in conformity with the powers delegated to me; and that I will to the utmost of my skill and ability, promote the peace and prosperity and maintain the lawful rights of the said State. So help me God.

                                              CHRIS CHRISTIE

Sworn to the 21st day of January 2014, and thereafter subscribed before me.

Christopher S. Porrino
Chief Counsel

A TRUE COPY
KIM GUADAGNO

SECRETARY OF STATE

185

LIEUTENANT GOVERNOR OF THE STATE OF NEW JERSEY

STATE OF NEW JERSEY }
                    } ss.
COUNTY OF MERCER   }

I, KIM GUADAGNO, do solemnly swear that I will support the Constitution of the United States and the Constitution of the State of New Jersey, and that I will bear true faith and allegiance to the same and to the Governments established in the United States, and in this State, under the authority of the people; and that I will faithfully, impartially and justly perform all the duties of the office of Lieutenant Governor according to the best of my ability. So help me God.

Sworn to the 21st day of January 2014, and thereafter subscribed before me.

Christopher S. Porrino
Chief Counsel

KIM GUADAGNO

A TRUE COPY
KIM GUADAGNO

SECRETARY OF STATE

186

STATE OF NEW JERSEY :
                          SS.
COUNTY OF Monmouth :

I, Kimberly M. Guadagno do solemnly swear (or affirm) that I will support the Constitution of the United States and the Constitution of the State of New Jersey; that I will bear true faith and allegiance to the same and to the Governments established in the United States and in this State, under the authority of the people; and that I will faithfully, impartially and justly perform all the duties of the office of Secretary of State

according to the best of my ability. *(So help me God)**

Sworn and subscribed to before me
this 21st day of January,
A.D. 2014

A TRUE COPY
KIM GUADAGNO

SECRETARY OF STATE

FILED

JAN 27 2014

KIM GUADAGNO
SECRETARY OF STATE

Person taking oath has the option of including "So help me God," if he/she so desires.

187

STATE OF NEW JERSEY

COUNTY OF MERCER

FEB - 3 20

USPS

I, **John J. Hoffman,** do solemnly swear that I will support the

Constitution of the United States and the Constitution of the State of New Jersey;

that I will bear true faith and allegiance to the same and to the Governments

established in the United States and in this State, under the authority of the people;

and that I will faithfully, impartially and justly perform all the duties of the office of

Acting Attorney General, according to the best of my ability. So help me God*.

John J. Hoffman

Sworn and subscribed to before me

this 19th day of July, 2013.

Chris Christie, Governor
State of New Jersey

A TRUE COPY
KIM GUADAGNO

SECRETARY OF STATE

FILED

JUL 1 9 2013

KIM GUADAGNO
SECRETARY OF STATE

*Person taking oath has the option of including "SO help me God," if he so desires.

OATH

I, _Bill Richardson_ , do solemnly swear that I will support the Constitution of the United States and the Constitution and the laws of the State of New Mexico and that I will faithfully and impartially discharge the duties of the office of _GOVERNOR of the State of N.M._ on which I am about to enter, to the best of my ability, SO HELP ME GOD.

Bill Richardson
APPOINTEE'S SIGNATURE

Subscribed and sworn to before me this _6th_ day of _January_ , 20_03_ .

Florence N. Witt
SIGNATURE

Notary Public
TITLE

My commission/term expires _4/05/03_

(This oath, when executed, must be forwarded immediately to the Secretary of State at Santa Fe, New Mexico, accompanied by a recording fee of $3.00.)

OATH

I,_____Bill Richardson_____, do solemnly swear that I will support the Constitution of the United States and the Constitution and laws of the State of New Mexico and that I will faithfully and impartially discharge the duties of the office of _____GOVERNOR OF THE STATE OF NEW MEXICO_____ on which I am about to enter, to the best of my ability, SO HELP ME GOD.

Bill Richardson

Appointee's Signature

OFFICIAL SEAL
Ed L. Romero
NOTARY PUBLIC
STATE OF NEW MEXICO
My Commission Expires: _____

Sworn and subscribed before me this _1st_

day of _____January_____, 20 _07_

Signature

(Seal)

_____Ed L. Romero, Notary Public_____
Title

My commission term expires _December 26, 2010_

190

Official State Flag

Oath

4451078

I _Susan Martinez_ , do solemnly swear that I will
support the Constitution of the United States and the Constitution
and the laws of the State of New Mexico and that I will faithfully
and impartially discharge the duties of the office
of _Governor_ on which I am
about to enter, to the best of my ability, SO HELP ME GOD.

_____ SIGNATURE

Subscribed and sworn to before me

this _1st_ day of _January_,

200_8_ .

[SEAL]

Robin M Buick
Notary Public

_____ SIGNATURE

_____ TITLE

My commission/term expires _5-9-12_

(This oath, when executed, must be forwarded immediately to the
Secretary of State at Santa Fe, New Mexico, accompanied by a
recording fee of $3.00.)

2011 JAN -3 AM 8:09

455860

Flag of the United States of the America
Title 4. U.S.A. Govern. Division 1, Section 1/6

OATH OF OFFICE
for
ELECTED OFFICIALS

STATE OF NEW MEXICO

COUNTY OF DOÑA ANA

Freedom
FOREVER

I, Susana Martinez, do solemnly swear that I will support and uphold the Constitution of the United States of America and the Constitution and Laws of the State of New Mexico, and that I will faithfully and impartially discharge the duties of the office of Third Judicial District Attorney, into which I am about to enter, to the best of my ability, so help me God.

Susana Martinez, Third Judicial District Attorney
December 31, 2004

Hon. Robert Robles, Third Judicial District Chief Judge
December 31, 2004

OATH

I, Hector Balderas, do solemnly swear that I will support the Constitution of the United States and the Constitution and the laws of the State of New Mexico and that I will faithfully and impartially discharge the duties of the office of Attorney General, on which I am about to enter, to the best of my ability, SO HELP ME GOD.

_____
SIGNATURE

Subscribed and sworn to before me on

this 3rd day of January,

2015.

_____
SIGNATURE

Justice, NMSC
_____
TITLE

My term expires: December 31, 2022

(This oath, when executed, must be forwarded immediately to the Secretary of State at Santa Fe, New Mexico, accompanied by a recording fee of $3.00)

Flag of the United States of the America
Title 4, U.S.A. Codes: Chapter 1: Section 142

State of New Mexico   }
                           } ss.
County of Torrance   }

OATH OF OFFICE

I, **Matthew "Mateo" S. Page,** do solemnly swear that I will support the Constitution of the United States and the Constitution and the laws of the State of New Mexico and that I will faithfully and impartially discharge all duties of the office of Magistrate Judge, Division I, for Torrance County, New Mexico, to the best of my ability, so help me God.

_____
Matthew "Mateo" S. Page

Subscribed and sworn before me on this 6th
day of December, 2014.

_____
The Honorable Buddy J. Hall
Magistrate Judge

Office of the Secretary of State
Dianna J. Duran

325 Don Gaspar, Suite 300, Santa Fe, NM 87503
Phone (505) 827-3600   Fax (505) 827-8403

FAX COVER SHEET

DATE: August 12, 2015

FAX NUMBER: 1-605-432-6479

PAGES: 1 including cover page

TO: Mr. Robert Simpson

FROM: Tracey Littrell

Official State Flag

I have gone through my files and find no Oath of Office for Clarence L. Gibson, former Torrance County Sheriff.

Thank you,
Tracey Littrell

TOTAL P.01

Office of the Secretary of State
Dianna J. Duran

325 Don Gaspar, Suite 300, Santa Fe, NM 87503
Phone (505) 827-3600   Fax (505) 827-8403

FAX COVER SHEET

DATE: August 13, 2015   Official State Flag

FAX NUMBER: 1-605-432-6479

PAGES: 1 including cover page

TO: Mr. Robert Simpson

FROM: Tracey Littrell

I have gone through my files and find no Oath of Office for the current or former Torrance County Sheriff, and I find no Oath of Office for the current or former Torrance County Manager.

Thank you,
Tracey Littrell

OATH OF OFFICE

I, Andrew M. Cuomo, do solemnly swear that I will support the constitution of the United States, and the constitution of the State of New York, and that I will faithfully discharge the duties of the office of Governor of the State of New York, according to the best of my ability.

Andrew M. Cuomo

Sworn to before me this
27th day of December, 2010

Notary Public

STATE OF NEW YORK
DEPARTMENT OF STATE
FILED

DEC 3 0 2010

MISCELLANEOUS
& STATE RECORDS

LISA D CANTWELL
NOTARY PUBLIC STATE OF NEW YORK
NASSAU COUNTY LIC. #01CA...
COMM. EXP NOVEMBER 14, 20...

PUBLIC OFFICER
OATH/AFFIRMATION

Flag of the United States of the America
Title: 4 U.S.A. Codes: Chapter: to Section 152

(TYPE ALL INFORMATION -- SIGN IN BLACK INK)

Name of Appointee: Hochul   Kathleen   C.

              (Last Name)   (First Name)   (Middle Initial)

STATE OF NEW YORK   )
) ss.:
COUNTY OF Albany   )

I do solemnly swear (or affirm) that I will support the constitution of the United States, and the constitution of the State of New York, and that I will faithfully discharge the duties of the office of

Title of Position:
Lieutenant Governor

Agency Name:
Office of the Lieutenant Governor

Agency Code: 01040

according to the best of my ability.

X _Kathleen C. Hochul_
(Signature of Appointee)

Sworn (or affirmed) before me this _3/st_ day

of _December_ , in the year, 20 _14_

Michelle P. Clark
Notary Public

****

PUBLIC OFFICERS LAW §78 CERTIFICATE

I, the Appointee named above, hereby acknowledge receipt of a copy of sections 73, 73-a, 74, 75, 76, 77 and 78 of the Public Officers Law, together with such other material related thereto as may have been prepared by the Secretary of State, and I acknowledge that I have read the same and that I undertake to conform to the provisions, purposes and intent thereof and to the norms of conduct for members, officers and employees of the legislature and state agencies.

X _Kathleen C. Hochul_   December 31, 2014
(Signature of Appointee)   (Date)

**(Appointee must sign both the Public Officer Oath/Affirmation
and the Public Officers Law §78 Certificate)**

DOS-1750-H (Rev. 09/14)   Go to www.dos.ny.gov for filing instructions.

Flag of the United States of the America
Title: 4, U.S.A. Codes, Chapter: 1; Section: 102

PUBLIC OFFICER
OATH/AFFIRMATION

Name of Appointee: Perales   Cesar
     (Last Name)   (First Name)

STATE OF NEW YORK   )
) ss:
COUNTY OF Albany   )

Insert the name of the County within New York State in which this Oath is being executed. Please note that ss: does not stand for "social security." The appointee's social security number should NOT be inserted anywhere on this form.

I do solemnly swear (or affirm) that I will support the constitution of the United States, and the constitution of the State of New York, and that I will faithfully discharge the duties of the office of

Title of Position:

  Secretary of State

Agency Name:

  Department of State

Agency Code: 19000

according to the best of my ability.

(Signature of Appointee)

Sworn (or affirmed) before me this 7th

day of June , in the year, 20 11

Notary Public

NANCY L. NEMETH
Notary Public, State of New York
No. 01NE6003444
Qualified in Albany County,
Commission Expires June 29, 20__

****

PUBLIC OFFICERS LAW §78 CERTIFICATE

I, the Appointee named above, hereby acknowledge receipt of a copy of sections 73, 73-a, 74, 75, 76, 77 and 78 of the Public Officers Law, together with such other material related thereto as may have been prepared by the Secretary of State, and I acknowledge that I have read the same and that I undertake to conform to the provisions, purposes and intent thereof and to the norms of conduct for members, officers and employees of the legislature and state agencies.

(Signature of Appointee)   *(Date)* June 7, 2011

**(Appointee must sign both the Public Officer Oath/Affirmation
and the Public Officer's Law §78 Certificate)**

DOS-1750 (Rev. 02/09)

199

PUBLIC OFFICER
OATH/AFFIRMATION

(TYPE ALL INFORMATION – SIGN IN BLACK INK)

Name of Appointee: Schneiderman, Eric T.

(Last Name) (First Name) (Middle Initial)

STATE OF NEW YORK ）
) ss.:
COUNTY OF New York ）

I do solemnly swear (or affirm) that I will support the constitution of the United States, and the constitution of the State of New York, and that I will faithfully discharge the duties of the office of

**FILED
STATE RECORDS**

Title of Position:

Attorney General of the State of New York

DEC 19 2014

DEPARTMENT OF STATE

Agency Name:

Office of the Attorney General

Agency Code: 01050

according to the best of my ability.

X _____
(Signature of Appointee)

Sworn (or affirmed) before me this ___18th___ day

of __DECEMBER__ , in the year, 20 _14_ .

_____
Notary Public

ALEXANDER C RABB
NOTARY PUBLIC STATE OF NEW YORK
KINGS COUNTY
LIC. #02RA6239444
COMM. EXP. April 18, 2015

****

PUBLIC OFFICERS LAW §78 CERTIFICATE

I, the Appointee named above, hereby acknowledge receipt of a copy of sections 73, 73-a, 74, 75, 76, 77 and 78 of the Public Officers Law, together with such other material related thereto as may have been prepared by the Secretary of State, and I acknowledge that I have read the same and that I undertake to conform to the provisions, purposes and intent thereof and to the norms of conduct for members, officers and employees of the legislature and state agencies.

X _____   __12/18/14__
(Signature of Appointee)   (Date)

**(Appointee must sign both the Public Officer Oath/Affirmation
and the Public Officers Law §78 Certificate)**

DOS-1760-f-l (Rev. 08/14)

Go to www.dos.ny.gov for filing instructions.

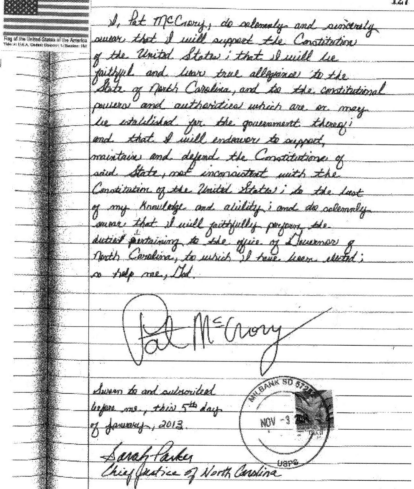

I, Pat McCrory, do solemnly and sincerely swear that I will support the Constitution of the United States; that I will be faithful and bear true allegiance to the State of North Carolina, and to the constitutional powers and authorities which are or may be established for the government thereof; and that I will endeavor to support, maintain and defend the Constitution of said State, not inconsistent with the Constitution of the United States; to the best of my knowledge and ability; and do solemnly swear that I will faithfully perform the duties pertaining to the office of Governor of North Carolina, to which I have been elected; so help me, God.

Pat McCrory

Sworn to and subscribed before me, this 5th day of January, 2013.

Sarah Parker
Chief Justice of North Carolina

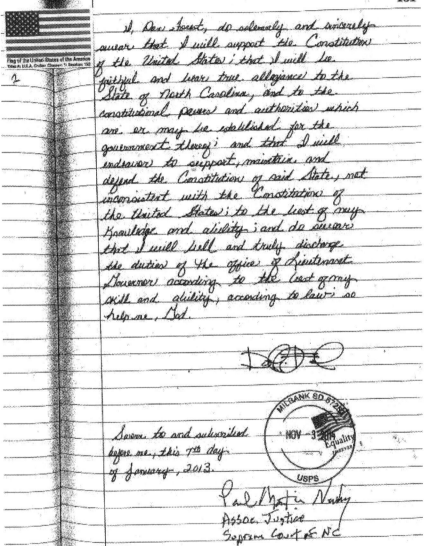

I, Dan Forest, do solemnly and sincerely swear that I will support the Constitution of the United States; that I will be faithful and bear true allegiance to the State of North Carolina, and to the constitutional powers and authorities which are or may be established for the government thereof; and that I will endeavor to support, maintain and defend the Constitution of said State, not inconsistent with the Constitution of the United States; to the best of my knowledge and ability; and do swear that I will well and truly discharge the duties of the office of Lieutenant Governor according to the best of my skill and ability, according to law; so help me, God.

Sworn to and subscribed before me, this 7th day of January, 2013.

Paul Martin Newby
Assoc. Justice
Supreme Court of NC

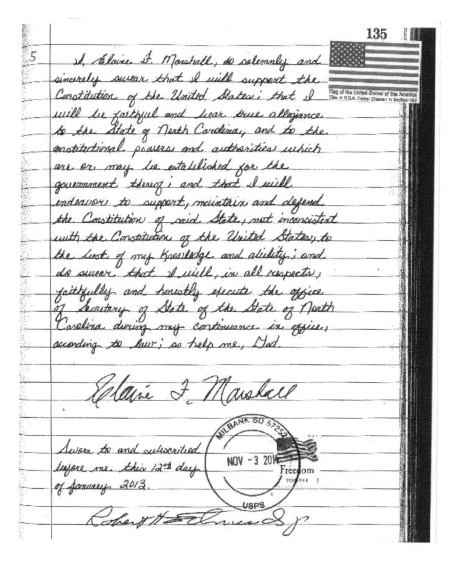

5

I, Elaine F. Marshall, do solemnly and sincerely swear that I will support the Constitution of the United States; that I will be faithful and bear true allegiance to the State of North Carolina, and to the constitutional powers and authorities which are or may be established for the government thereof; and that I will endeavor to support, maintain and defend the Constitution of said State, not inconsistent with the Constitution of the United States, to the best of my knowledge and ability; and do swear that I will, in all respects, faithfully and honestly execute the office of Secretary of State of the State of North Carolina during my continuance in office, according to law; so help me, God.

Elaine F. Marshall

Sworn to and subscribed before me this 12th day of January, 2013.

Robert H. Brown Jr.

135

I, Roy Cooper, do solemnly and sincerely swear that I will support the Constitution of the United States; that I will be faithful and bear true allegiance to the State of North Carolina, and to the constitutional powers and authorities which are or may be established for the government thereof; and that I will endeavor to support, maintain and defend the Constitution of said State, not inconsistent with the Constitution of the United States, to the best of my knowledge and ability; and do solemnly swear that I will well and truly serve the State of North Carolina in the office of Attorney General and I will, in the execution of my office, endeavor to have the criminal laws fairly and impartially administered, as far as in me lies, according to the best of my knowledge and ability; so help me, God.

Roy Cooper

Sworn to and subscribed
before me this 12th day
of January 2013.

204

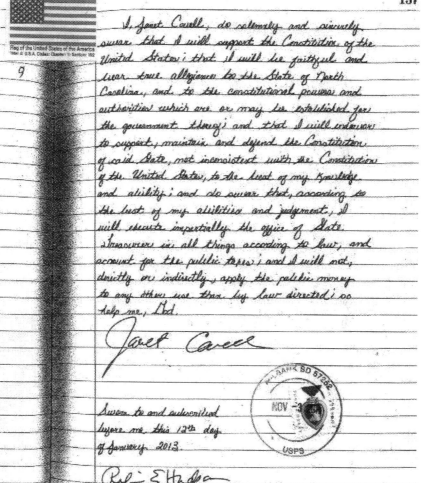

I, Janet Cowell, do solemnly and sincerely swear that I will support the Constitution of the United States; that I will be faithful and bear true allegiance to the State of North Carolina, and to the constitutional powers and authorities which are or may be established for the government thereof; and that I will endeavor to support, maintain and defend the Constitution of said State, not inconsistent with the Constitution of the United States, to the best of my knowledge and ability; and do swear that, according to the best of my abilities and judgement, I will execute impartially the office of State Treasurer in all things according to law, and account for the public taxes; and I will not, directly or indirectly, apply the public money to any other use than by law directed; so help me, God.

Janet Cowell

Sworn to and subscribed before me, this 12th day of January, 2013.

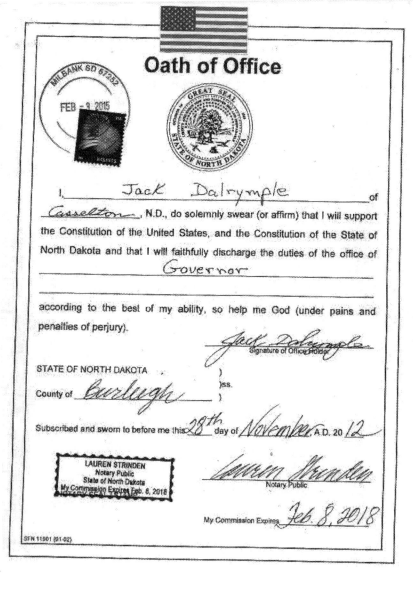

Oath of Office

I, *Jack Dalrymple* of *Casselton*, N.D., do solemnly swear (or affirm) that I will support the Constitution of the United States, and the Constitution of the State of North Dakota and that I will faithfully discharge the duties of the office of *Governor*

according to the best of my ability, so help me God (under pains and penalties of perjury).

Jack Dalrymple
Signature of Office Holder

STATE OF NORTH DAKOTA)
)ss.
County of *Burleigh*)

Subscribed and sworn to before me this *28th* day of *November* A.D. 20 *12*

LAUREN STRINDEN
Notary Public
State of North Dakota
My Commission Expires Feb. 8, 2018

Lauren Strinden
Notary Public

My Commission Expires *Feb. 8, 2018*

SFN 11901 (01-02)

206

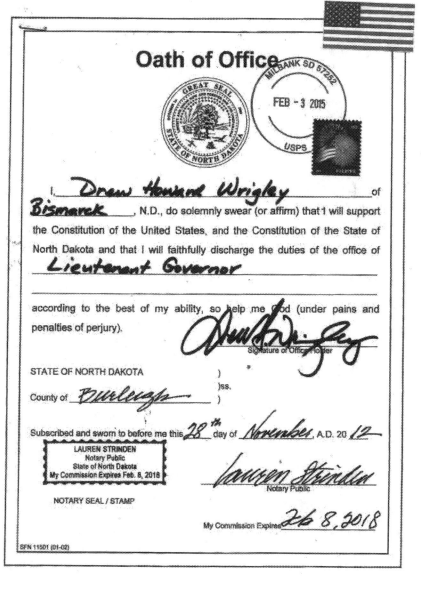

Oath of Office

I, _Drew Howard Wrigley_ of
Bismarck, N.D., do solemnly swear (or affirm) that I will support
the Constitution of the United States, and the Constitution of the State of
North Dakota and that I will faithfully discharge the duties of the office of
Lieutenant Governor

according to the best of my ability, so help me God (under pains and
penalties of perjury).

_____
Signature of Office Holder

STATE OF NORTH DAKOTA)
)ss.
County of _Burleigh_   )

Subscribed and sworn to before me this _28th_ day of _November_, A.D. 20 _12_

LAUREN STRINDEN
Notary Public
State of North Dakota
My Commission Expires Feb. 8, 2018

_____
Notary Public

NOTARY SEAL / STAMP

My Commission Expires _Feb 8, 2018_

SFN 11501 (01-02)

207

Oath of Office

I, _Alvin A Jaeger_ of

Bismarck , N.D., do solemnly swear (or affirm) that I will support the Constitution of the United States, and the Constitution of the State of North Dakota and that I will faithfully discharge the duties of the office of

Secretary of State

according to the best of my ability, so help me God (under pains and penalties of perjury).

Signature of Office Holder

STATE OF NORTH DAKOTA   )
)ss.
County of _Burleigh_   )

Subscribed and sworn to before me this _21st_ day of _November_ , A.D. 20 _14_

Notary Public

LEE ANN OLIVER
Notary Public
NOTARY SEAL / STAMP
State of North Dakota
My Commission Expires April 12, 2015

My Commission Expires_____

SFN 11501 (01-02)

208

Oath of Office

I, ____Wayne Stenehjem_____ of

___Bismarck_____, N.D., do solemnly swear (or affirm) that I will support

the Constitution of the United States, and the Constitution of the State of

North Dakota and that I will faithfully discharge the duties of the office of

___Attorney General_____

_____

according to the best of my ability, so help me God (under pains and

penalties of perjury).

_____
Signature of Office Holder

STATE OF NORTH DAKOTA   )
)ss.
County of Burleigh   )

Subscribed and sworn to before me this 24 day of December, A.D. 2014

_____
Notary Public

NOTARY SEAL / STAMP

My Commission Expires

ELIZABETH BROCKER
Notary Public
State of North Dakota
My Commission Expires Dec. 22, 2016

SFN 11501 (01-02)

209

O's

Ohio
Oklahoma
Oregon

OATH OF OFFICE

I, John Richard Kasich, do solemnly swear, that I shall faithfully, and honestly, discharge the duties of the office of Governor of Ohio, and shall support, protect and defend the Constitution of the United States and the Constitution of the State of Ohio, so help me God.

John Richard Kasich

STATE OF OHIO
COUNTY OF FRANKLIN

Personally sworn to before me, Maureen O'Connor, Chief Justice, Supreme Court of Ohio, and subscribed to my presence this 10th day of January, 2011.

Maureen O'Connor, Chief Justice
Supreme Court of Ohio

OATH OF OFFICE

I, Mary Taylor, do solemnly swear that I shall faithfully and honestly discharge the duties of the office of Lieutenant Governor of the State of Ohio, and shall support, protect and defend the Constitution of the United States of America and the Constitution of the State of Ohio, so help me God.

Mary Taylor

STATE OF OHIO
COUNTY OF FRANKLIN

Personally sworn to before me, Maureen O'Connor, Chief Justice, Supreme Court of Ohio, and subscribed to my presence this 10th day of January, 2011.

Maureen O'Connor, Chief Justice
Supreme Court of Ohio

OATH OF OFFICE

I, Richard Michael DeWine, do solemnly swear, that I shall faithfully and honestly discharge the duties of the office of Ohio Attorney General; that I shall preserve, protect, and defend the Constitution of the United States and the Constitution of the State of Ohio; that I shall seek truth and justice; and that I shall do everything in my power to protect Ohio families -- so help me God.

Richard Michael DeWine

STATE OF OHIO
County of Franklin

Personally sworn to before me, a Notary Public in and for said County, and subscribed to in my presence this 9th Day of January, 2011.

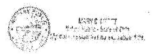

Notary Public

213

FILED

JAN 12 2015

OATH OF OFFICE
(Art. XV O.C. §1)

OKLAHOMA SECRETARY
OF STATE

I, _____ Mary Fallin _____, do solemnly swear (or affirm) that I will support, obey, and defend the Constitution of the United States, and the Constitution of the State of Oklahoma, and that I will not, knowingly, receive, directly or indirectly, any money or other valuable thing, for the performance or nonperformance of any act or duty pertaining to my office, other than the compensation allowed by law; I further swear (or affirm) that I will faithfully discharge my duties as

_____ Governor of the State of Oklahoma _____

to the best of my ability.

State of _____ Oklahoma _____

County of _____ Oklahoma _____

Affiant Sign Here

Signed and sworn to (or affirmed) before me on this ___12th___ day of _____ January _____, __2015__ by

_____ Mary Fallin _____
Print name of person taking the oath

Signature of Notary

(Seal if any)

Commission Expires _____ X _____

Commission Number _____ X _____

_____ Justice _____
Title and Rank (if other than a notary)

(9/2003)

FILED

OATH OF OFFICE
(Art. XV O.C. §1)

OKLAHOMA SECRETARY
OF STATE

I, _TODD GRIFFIN LAMB_ , do solemnly swear (or affirm) that I will support, obey, and defend the Constitution of the United States, and the Constitution of the State of Oklahoma, and that I will not, knowingly, receive, directly or indirectly, any money or other valuable thing, for the performance or nonperformance of any act or duty pertaining to my office, other than the compensation allowed by law; I further swear (or affirm) that I will faithfully discharge my duties as

LIEUTENANT GOVERNOR
to the best of my ability.

_____
Affiant Sign Here

State of _OKLAHOMA_

County of _OKLAHOMA_

Signed and sworn to (or affirmed) before me on this _12th_ day of _January_, _2015_ by

TODD GRIFFIN LAMB
Print name of person taking the oath

_____
Signature of the Notary

(Seal if any)

Commission Expires _July 13, 2017_

Commission Number _05006391_

_____
Title and Rank (if other than a notary)
notary

(9/2003)

FILED

JAN 12 2015
OKLAHOMA SECRETARY
OF STATE

OATH OF OFFICE
(Art. XV O.C. §1)

I, __G. Chris Benge__ , do solemnly swear (or affirm) that I will support, obey, and defend the Constitution of the United States, and the Constitution of the State of Oklahoma, and that I will not, knowingly, receive, directly or indirectly, any money or other valuable thing, for the performance or nonperformance of any act or duty pertaining to my office, other than the compensation allowed by law; I further swear (or affirm) that I will faithfully discharge my duties as

Secretary of State

to the best of my ability.

State of __OKLAHOMA__

County of __OKLAHOMA__

Affiant Sign Here

Signed and sworn to (or affirmed) before me on this __12th__ day of __January__, __2015__ by

__G. Chris Benge__
Print name of person taking the oath

Signature of the Notary

(Seal if any)

Commission Expires _____

Title and Rank (if other than a notary)

Commission Number _____

(9/2005)

RECEIVED

JAN 1 2 2015

OKLAHOMA SECRETARY
OF STATE

216

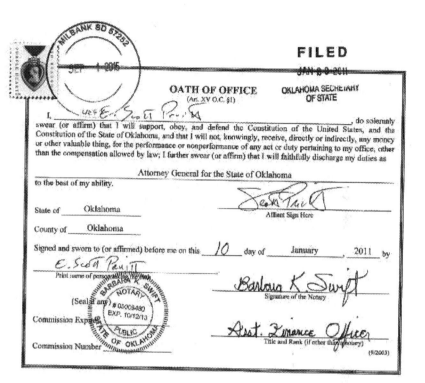

FILED

OATH OF OFFICE
(Art. XV O.C. §1)

I, _____, do solemnly swear (or affirm) that I will support, obey, and defend the Constitution of the United States, and the Constitution of the State of Oklahoma, and that I will not, knowingly, receive, directly or indirectly, any money or other valuable thing, for the performance or nonperformance of any act or duty pertaining to my office, other than the compensation allowed by law; I further swear (or affirm) that I will faithfully discharge my duties as

Attorney General for the State of Oklahoma

to the best of my ability.

State of _____ Oklahoma

County of _____ Oklahoma

_____
Affiant Sign Here

Signed and sworn to (or affirmed) before me on this ___10___ day of _____ January _____, 2011 by

E. Scott Pruitt
Print name of person

(Seal if any)

Commission Expires

Commission Number

_____
Signature of the Notary

_____
Title and Rank (if other than notary)

(9/2003)

AP 205-0039

FILED

STATE OF OREGON
OATH OF OFFICE

State of Oregon
County of Marion
} ss

I, *JOHN KITZHABER*, do solemnly swear or affirm, that I will support the Constitution of the United States, and the Constitution of the State of Oregon, and that I will faithfully discharge the duties of

GOVERNOR

according to the best of my ability.

_____
John Kitzhaber

Subscribed and sworn to, or affirmed, before me
this 12th day of January, 2015.

_____
The Honorable Paul J. DeMuniz
State of Oregon, Retired

A.P 2013-0032

STATE OF OREGON
OATH OF OFFICE

State of Oregon
County of Marion } ss

I, *ELLEN ROSENBLUM*, *do solemnly swear, or affirm, that I will support the Constitution of the United States, and the Constitution of the State of Oregon, and that I will faithfully discharge the duties of*

ATTORNEY GENERAL

according to the best of my ability.

Ellen Rosenblum

Subscribed and sworn to, or affirmed, before me
this __18__ day of __March__, 20 _13_.

_____
Notary Public for Oregon, or Judicial Title
My commission/term expires: _3-12-2017_

OFFICIAL SEAL
CHRYSTAL M BADER
NOTARY PUBLIC-OREGON
COMMISSION NO. 475446
MY COMMISSION EXPIRES MARCH 12, 2017

P
Pennsylvania

Commonwealth of Pennsylvania

Constitutional Oath of Office

Commonwealth of Pennsylvania

ss:

County of Dauphin

I, Thomas Westerman Wolf, do solemnly swear that I will support, obey and defend the Constitution of the United States and the Constitution of this Commonwealth and that I will discharge the duties of my office with fidelity.

Thomas Westerman Wolf

Sworn and subscribed before me, this twentieth day of January A.D. 2015.

The Honorable Renee Blackwell
Judge of the Court of Common Pleas

Constitutional Oath of Office

Commonwealth of Pennsylvania

ss:

County of Dauphin

I, Jim Cawley, do solemnly swear (or affirm) that I will support, obey and defend the Constitution of the United States and the Constitution of this Commonwealth and that I will discharge the duties of the office of Lieutenant Governor with fidelity.

Jim Cawley

Taken, sworn and subscribed before me this eighteenth day of January, A.D. 2011.

D. Michael Fisher
Judge
United States Court of Appeals
Third Circuit

222

Constitutional Oath of Office

Commonwealth of Pennsylvania

ss:

County of Dauphin

I, Kathleen G. Kane, do solemnly swear (or affirm) that I will support, obey and defend the Constitution of the United States and the Constitution of this Commonwealth and that I will discharge the duties of my office with fidelity.

_____
Kathleen G. Kane

Taken, sworn and subscribed before me this fifteenth day of January, A.D. 2013.

_____
Margaret A. Bisignani Moyle
Judge of the Court of Common Pleas
Lackawanna County

RECEIVED
2013 JAN 17 PM 1:4
Department of State
Bureau of C.E.L.

223

COMMONWEALTH OF PENNSYLVANIA

CONSTITUTIONAL OATH OF OFFICE

COMMONWEALTH OF PENNSYLVANIA)

) SS

County of Dauphin)

I do solemnly swear (or affirm) that I will support, obey and defend the Constitution of the United States and the Constitution of the Commonwealth of Pennsylvania and that I will discharge the duties of my office with fidelity.

_____
SIGNATURE OF OFFICER

Pedro A. Cortés
NAME OF OFFICER

Secretary, Department of State
OFFICER TITLE

Taken, sworn and subscribed before me this 27th day of July, A.D. 2015.

_____
Signature of Person Administering Oath

(Notary Seal, if applicable)

****

NOTE: The foregoing oath shall be administered by some person authorized to administer oaths.

The oaths of STATE OFFICERS, JUSTICES OF THE SUPREME COURT and JUDGES OF THE SUPERIOR AND COMMONWEALTH COURTS shall be filed in the office of the Secretary of the Commonwealth.

The oaths of other judicial and county officers shall be filed with the Prothonotary of the county in which the oath is taken.

DSCB-7

R

Rhode Island

2015 JAN -9 AM 10: 54

STATE OF RHODE ISLAND AND PROVIDENCE PLANTATIONS

ELECTED OFFICIALS

CERTIFICATE OF ENGAGEMENT

Certificate to be filled out and delivered to the Secretary of State within THIRTY (30) DAYS after the date of Commission pursuant to §36-1-4 of the General Laws of Rhode Island.

___Providence___ County in the ___City___ of ___Providence___

and the County and State aforesaid, on the __6th__ day of ___January___ _2015_

I, ___Gina M. Raimondo___ hereby make oath to support the Constitution and

Laws of this State, and the Constitution of the United States, and faithfully and impartially to

discharge according to the best of my abilities the duties, of the office of:

___Governor___

Signed: _____

Address: ___125 Morris Ave.,___

___Providence, RI 02906___

Telephone: ___(401)529-6048___

Dated: _January 6, 2015_

Signed before me, this __6__ day of _January_ , 20_15_

Donna M. DeLl'Aquila

Expires: _April 15, 2015_

226

STATE OF RHODE ISLAND AND PROVIDENCE PLANTATIONS

ELECTED OFFICIALS

CERTIFICATE OF ENGAGEMENT

Certificate to be filled out and delivered to the Secretary of State within THIRTY (30) DAYS after the date of Commission pursuant to §36-1-4 of the General Laws of Rhode Island.

_____ Providence _____ County in the _____ City _____ of _____ Providence _____

and the County and State aforesaid, on the __6th__ day of _____ January _____ 2015 _____

I, _____ Daniel J. Mckee _____ hereby make oath to support the Constitution and

Laws of this State, and the Constitution of the United States, and faithfully and impartially to

discharge according to the best of my abilities the duties, of the office of:

_____ Lieutenant Governor _____

Signed: _____

Address: _____ 12 Hillside Rd. _____

_____ Cumberland, RI 02864 _____

Telephone: _____ 401- 465-6204 _____

Dated: 1-7-15

Signed before me, this __7__ day of __January__ , 20 __15__

_____

Expires: 8-15-18

227

Flag of the United States of the America
Title 4: U.S.A. Codes: Chapter 1: Section 162

2015 JAN 12 PM 4:19

2015 JAN 12 PM 4:21

STATE OF RHODE ISLAND AND PROVIDENCE PLANTATIONS

ELECTED OFFICIALS

CERTIFICATE OF ENGAGEMENT

Certificate to be filled out and delivered to the Secretary of State within THIRTY (30) DAYS after the date of Commission pursuant to §36-1-4 of the General Laws of Rhode Island.

___Providence___ County in the ___City___ of ___Providence___

and the County and State aforesaid, on the _6th_ day of ___January___ _2015_

I, ___Nellie M. Gorbea___ hereby make oath to support the Constitution and

Laws of this State, and the Constitution of the United States, and faithfully and impartially to

discharge according to the best of my abilities the duties, of the office of:

___Secretary Of State___

Signed: _____

Address: ___65 Fishing Cove Rd.,___

___North Kingstown, RI 02852___

Telephone: ___* (401)667-3656___

Dated: _1/13/2015_

Signed before me, this _12th_ day of _January_, 20_15_

_____

Expires: _02/04/2015_

Flag of the United States of the America
Title 4: U.S.A. Codes; Chapter: To Session: 162

2015 JAN -9 PM 3: 30

STATE OF RHODE ISLAND AND PROVIDENCE PLANTATIONS

ELECTED OFFICIALS

CERTIFICATE OF ENGAGEMENT

Certificate to be filled out and delivered to the Secretary of State within THIRTY (30) DAYS after the date of Commission pursuant to §36-1-4 of the General Laws of Rhode Island.

_____ Providence _____ County in the ____ City ____ of ____ Providence ____

and the County and State aforesaid, on the __8th__ day of ____ January ____ 2015 __

I, ___ Peter F. Kilmartin ___ hereby make oath to support the Constitution and

Laws of this State, and the Constitution of the United States, and faithfully and impartially to

discharge according to the best of my abilities the duties, of the office of:

_____ Attorney General _____

Signed: _____

Address: ____ 598 Armistice Blvd. ____

____ Pawtucket, RI 02861 ____

Telephone: ' (401)475-6059

Dated: 1/6/2015

Signed before me, this 6'th day of January , 20 15

MONICA A. NASON
ID # 753008
Expires: ____ NOTARY PUBLIC OF RHODE ISLAND
My Commission Expires 5/31/2015

229

STATE OF RHODE ISLAND AND PROVIDENCE PLANTATIONS

ELECTED OFFICIALS

CERTIFICATE OF ENGAGEMENT

Certificate to be filled out and delivered to the Secretary of State within THIRTY (30) DAYS after the
date of Commission pursuant to §36-1-4 of the General Laws of Rhode Island.

_____Providence_____ County in the _____City_____ of _____Providence_____

and the County and State aforesaid, on the __8th__ day of _____January_____ 2015

I, _____Seth Magaziner_____ hereby make oath to support the Constitution and

Laws of this State, and the Constitution of the United States, and faithfully and impartially to

discharge according to the best of my abilities the duties, of the office of:

_____General Treasurer_____

Signed: _____[signature]_____

Address: _____90 Eddy St. 303_____

_____Providence, RI 02903_____

Telephone: _____401-580-1442_____

Dated: __1/7/2015__

Signed before me, this __7th__ day of __January__, 20__15__

_____[signature]_____ # 753687

Expires: __1/26/2016__

S's

South Carolina

South Dakota

OATH FOR COUNTY AND STATE OFFICERS

1. *Immediately* return this completed, notarized oath form to:

    JAN 0 9 2015

    The Honorable Mark Hammond
    Office of the Secretary of State
    1205 Pendleton Street, Suite 525
    Columbia, South Carolina 29201
    Attn: Patricia Hamby, Director of Boards and Commissions

    SECRETARY OF STATE, SOUTH CAROLINA

2. *Print* your name, the office to which you have been appointed/elected, and your
    Mailing address plainly. *Make each letter plain and distinct.*

    PRINT NAME: __Nikki Randhawa Haley__

    APPOINTED/ELECTED: __Governor__
    (Name of Board, Commission or Position)

    MAILING ADDRESS: __1205 Pendleton Street; Columbia, SC 29201__

    TERM TO EXPIRE: __January 2015__

State of South Carolina
County of __RICHLAND__

First, I do solemnly swear (or affirm) that I am duly qualified, according, to the Constitution of this State, to
exercise the duties of the office to which I have been elected (or appointed), and that I will, to the best of my
ability, discharge the duties thereof, and preserve and protect and defend the Constitution of this State and of the
United States.

So help me God.

Signature of Appointed/Elected Official
Chief Justice of South Carolina
My commission expires
7-1-2014

Sworn to and subscribed before me this

__12th__ day of __Jan.__ __2011__

Notary Public of South Carolina
Robert M. Sisk
My Commission Expires __12-17-2020__

232

OATH FOR COUNTY AND STATE OFFICERS

1. *Immediately* return this completed, notarized oath form to:

The Honorable Mark Hammond
Office of the Secretary of State
1205 Pendleton Street, Suite 525
Columbia, South Carolina 29201
Attn: Tracy Sharpe, Director of Boards and Commissions

JAN 0 9 2015

SECRETARY OF STATE OF SOUTH CAROLINA

2. *Print* your name, the office to which you have been appointed/elected, and your mailing address plainly. *Make each letter plain and distinct.*

PRINT NAME: ___Henry Dargan McMaster___

APPOINTED/ELECTED: ___Lieutenant Governor___
(Name of Board, Commission or Position)

MAILING ADDRESS: _Post Office Box 11063 Columbia, South Carolina_ 29211

TERM TO EXPIRE: _January 9, 2019_

State of South Carolina
County of _Richland_

First, I do solemnly swear (or affirm) that I am duly qualified, according, to the Constitution of this State, to exercise the duties of the office to which I have been elected (or appointed), and that I will, to the best of my ability, discharge the duties thereof, and preserve and protect and defend the Constitution of this State and of the United States.

So help me God.

_____
Signature of Appointed/Elected Official

Sworn to and subscribed before me this

_3rd_ , day of _December_ , 2014

_____
Notary Public of South Carolina
Owen K. Kittrell
My Commission Expires _6/26/17_

233

OATH FOR COUNTY AND STATE OFFICERS

1. _Immediately_ return this completed, notarized oath form to:

The Honorable Mark Hammond
Office of the Secretary of State
1205 Pendleton Street, Suite 525
Columbia, South Carolina 29201
Attn: Tracy Sharpe, Director of Boards and Commissions

JAN 0 9 2015

SECRETARY OF STATE OF SOUTH CAROLINA

2. _Print_ your name, the office to which you have been appointed/elected, and your mailing address plainly. _Make each letter plain and distinct._

PRINT NAME: ALAN WILSON

APPOINTED/ELECTED: ATTORNEY GENERAL
(Name of Board, Commission or Position)

MAILING ADDRESS: 1000 ASSEMBLY STREET, ROOM 519
COLUMBIA, SOUTH CAROLINA 29201

TERM TO EXPIRE: JANUARY 8, 2019

State of South Carolina
County of RICHLAND

First, I do solemnly swear (or affirm) that I am duly qualified, according, to the Constitution of this State, to exercise the duties of the office to which I have been elected (or appointed), and that I will, to the best of my ability, discharge the duties thereof, and preserve and protect and defend the Constitution of this State and of the United States.

So help me God.

Signature of Appointed/Elected Official

Sworn to and subscribed before me this

25th day of November 20 14

Notary Public of South Carolina

My Commission Expires April 1, 2020

234

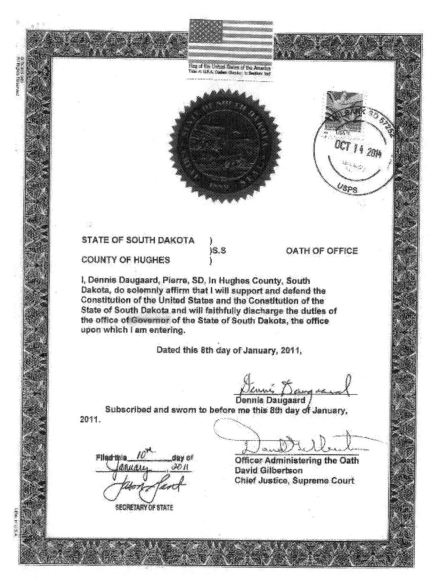

STATE OF SOUTH DAKOTA)
)S.S   OATH OF OFFICE
COUNTY OF HUGHES   )

I, Dennis Daugaard, Pierre, SD, in Hughes County, South Dakota, do solemnly affirm that I will support and defend the Constitution of the United States and the Constitution of the State of South Dakota and will faithfully discharge the duties of the office of Governor of the State of South Dakota, the office upon which I am entering.

Dated this 8th day of January, 2011,

Dennis Daugaard

Subscribed and sworn to before me this 8th day of January, 2011.

Officer Administering the Oath
David Gilbertson
Chief Justice, Supreme Court

Filed this 10th day of January, 2011

SECRETARY OF STATE

STATE OF SOUTH DAKOTA   )
)S.S   OATH OF OFFICE
COUNTY OF HUGHES   )

I, Matt Michels, Pierre, SD, in Hughes County, South
Dakota, do solemnly affirm that I will support and defend the
Constitution of the United States and the Constitution of the
State of South Dakota and will faithfully discharge the duties of
the office of Lieutenant Governor of the State of South Dakota, the
office upon which I am entering.

Dated this 8th day of January, 2011.

Matt Michels

Subscribed and sworn to before me this 8th day of January,
2011.

Filed this ___10th___ day of
___January___, 2011

SECRETARY OF STATE

Officer Administering the Oath
David Gilbertson
Chief Justice, Supreme Court

236

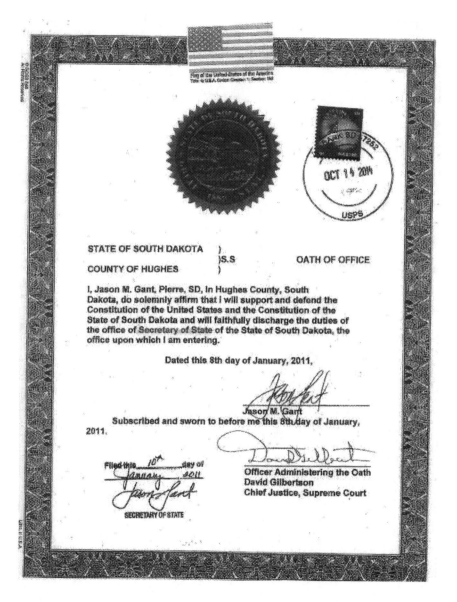

Flag of the United States of the America
Title: 4 U.S.A. Codon Chapter 1: Section 1&2

STATE OF SOUTH DAKOTA)
)S.S   OATH OF OFFICE
COUNTY OF HUGHES)

I, Jason M. Gant, Pierre, SD, in Hughes County, South
Dakota, do solemnly affirm that I will support and defend the
Constitution of the United States and the Constitution of the
State of South Dakota and will faithfully discharge the duties of
the office of Secretary of State of the State of South Dakota, the
office upon which I am entering.

Dated this 8th day of January, 2011,

Jason M. Gant

Subscribed and sworn to before me this 8th day of January,
2011.

Filed this __10th__ day of
__January__, __2011__

SECRETARY OF STATE

Officer Administering the Oath
David Gilbertson
Chief Justice, Supreme Court

STATE OF SOUTH DAKOTA)
)S.S   OATH OF OFFICE
COUNTY OF HUGHES   )

I, Marty J. Jackley, Pierre, SD, In Hughes County, South Dakota, do solemnly affirm that I will support and defend the Constitution of the United States and the Constitution of the State of South Dakota and will faithfully discharge the duties of the office of Attorney General of the State of South Dakota, the office upon which I am entering.

Dated this 8th day of January, 2011,

Marty J. Jackley

Subscribed and sworn to before me this 8th day of January, 2011.

Filed this 10ᵗʰ day of January, 2011

SECRETARY OF STATE

Officer Administering the Oath
David Gilbertson
Chief Justice, Supreme Court

Flag of the United States of the America
Title: 4: U.S.A. Cohen Chapter 1: Section 182

State of South Dakota

County of Hughes

I, Andy Gerlach, do solemnly swear that I will support the Constitution of the United States and the Constitution of the State of South Dakota, and that I will faithfully discharge the duties of the position of Secretary of the Department of Revenue.

Dated this 23 day of ___May___, 2011.

_____
Andy Gerlach

Subscribed and sworn to before me this

___23ᴿᴾ___ day of ___May___, 2011.

_____
Notary

My commission Expires:

___09-24-2014___

239

T's

Tennessee

Texas

STATE OF TENNESSEE

Oath of Office

I, **William Edward Haslam**, do solemnly swear that as Governor of the State of Tennessee, I will support the Constitution of the State of Tennessee and the Constitution of the United States, and that I will perform with fidelity and faithfully execute the duties of the office of Governor to which I have been elected and which I am about to assume, to the best of my skill and ability. So help me God.

This the 15th day of January, 2011.

_____

William Edward Haslam
GOVERNOR
STATE OF TENNESSEE

STATE OF TENNESSEE
COUNTY OF DAVIDSON

I, Cornelia A. Clark, Chief Justice of the Tennessee Supreme Court, have this day administered the Oath of Office to William Edward Haslam as Governor for the State of Tennessee as prescribed by law.

This the 15th day of January, 2011.

_____

Cornelia A. Clark
CHIEF JUSTICE
TENNESSEE SUPREME COURT

STATE OF TENNESSEE

Oath of Office

I, **Herbert H. Slatery III**, do solemnly swear that I will support the Constitution of the United States of America and the Constitution of the State of Tennessee, and I further swear that I will perform with fidelity the duties of the Office of Attorney General and Reporter for the State of Tennessee to which I have been appointed and to which I am about to assume.

So help me God.

This the 1st day of October, 2014.

_____
Herbert H. Slatery III

STATE OF TENNESSEE   )

COUNTY OF DAVIDSON   )

I, **Bill Haslam**, Governor of the State of Tennessee, and I, **Sharon G. Lee**, Chief Justice of the Tennessee Supreme Court, have this day administered the Oath of Office to Herbert H. Slatery III, Attorney General and Reporter of the State of Tennessee, as prescribed and required by law.

This the 1st day of October, 2014.

_____   _____
Sharon G. Lee   **Bill Haslam**

STATE OF TENNESSEE

Oath of Office

108th General Assembly

I, Tré Hargett, do solemnly swear that, as Secretary of State of the State of Tennessee, I will support the Constitution of the State of Tennessee and of the United States, and I will perform with fidelity and faithfully execute the duties of this office to the best of my ability.

So help me God.

Tré Hargett
Secretary of State

Ron Ramsey
Speaker of the Senate

Beth Harwell
Speaker of the House

Sworn and subscribed before me
at the Capitol, Nashville,
Tennessee, this the 9th day
of January, 2013

Justice William C. Koch, Jr.
Tennessee Supreme Court

Flag of the United States of the America
Title: 4; U.S.A. Codes; Chapter 1; Section 102

Form #2204   Rev. 10/2011

This space reserved for office
use

Submit to:
SECRETARY OF STATE
Government Filings Section
P O Box 12887
Austin, TX 78711-2887
512-463-5334

OATH OF OFFICE

Filing Fee: None

IN THE NAME AND BY THE AUTHORITY OF THE STATE OF TEXAS,

I, Gregory Wayne Abbott _____ , do solemnly swear (or affirm), that I will faithfully

execute the duties of the office of Governor _____ of

the State of Texas, and will to the best of my ability preserve, protect, and defend the Constitution and laws

of the United States and of this State, so help me God.

_____
Signature of Officer

State of   Texas   )
County of Travis   )

Sworn to and subscribed before me
this   21   day of January   20 15 .

(seal)

_____
Signature of Notary Public or Other Officer
Administering Oath
Chief Justice Nathan L. Hecht
Printed or Typed Name

MILBANK SD 57252

MAR 19 2015

USPS

Liberty
FOREVER

Form 2204   2

Form #2201 Rev. 10/2011	Flag of the United States of the America	This space reserved for office
	Title: 4; U.S.A. Codex Chapter 1; Section 182	use

Submit to:
SECRETARY OF STATE
Government Filings Section
P O Box 12887
Austin, TX 78711-2887
512-463-6334
512-463-5569 - Fax
Filing Fee: None

STATEMENT OF OFFICER

Filed in the Office of
Secretary of State

JAN 20 2015

GOVERNMENT
FILINGS SECTION

Statement

I, _____ Dan Patrick _____, do solemnly swear (or affirm) that I have not directly or indirectly paid, offered, promised to pay, contributed, or promised to contribute any money or thing of value, or promised any public office or employment for the giving or withholding of a vote at the election at which I was elected or as a reward to secure my appointment or confirmation, whichever the case may be, so help me God.

Position to Which Elected/Appointed: ___ Lieutenant Governor ___

City and/or County: ___ Houston, Harris County ___

Execution

Under penalties of perjury, I declare that I have read the foregoing statement and that the facts stated therein are true.

Date: ___ 1/20/2015 ___

_____
Signature of Officer

Revised 10/2011

Form 2201

2

OATH OF OFFICE

IN THE NAME AND BY THE AUTHORITY OF THE STATE OF TEXAS,

I, Ken Paxton, do solemnly swear (or affirm), that I will faithfully execute the duties of the office of the Attorney General of the State of Texas, and will to the best of my ability preserve, protect, and defend the Constitution and laws of the United States and of this State, so help me God.

Ken Paxton

Ken Paxton

Sworn to and Subscribed before me on this 5th day of January, 2015.

Greg Abbott

Greg Abbott
Former Attorney General and
Governor-Elect of Texas

246

U
Utah

Oath of Office

I, Gary R. Herbert, having been elected to the office of Governor, do solemnly swear that I will support, obey and defend the Constitution of the United States and the Constitution of this State and that I will discharge the duties of my office with fidelity.

Gary R. Herbert

Gary R. Herbert
Governor

Subscribed and Sworn to before me this seventh day of January two thousand and thirteen

Matthew B. Durrant

Matthew B. Durrant
Chief Justice, Utah Supreme Court

248

AUG 14 2015

I, Spencer J. Cox, having been appointed to the office of Lieutenant Governor, do solemnly swear that I will support, obey and defend the Constitution of the United States and the Constitution of this State and that I will discharge the duties of my office with fidelity.

Spencer J. Cox
Lieutenant Governor

Subscribed and Sworn to before me this sixteenth day of October, two thousand and thirteen

Ted Stewart
United States District Court Judge

Oath of Office

I, Sean David Reyes, having been elected to the office of Attorney General, do solemnly swear that I will support, obey and defend the Constitution of the United States and the Constitution of this State and that I will discharge the duties of my office with fidelity.

_____

Sean David Reyes
Attorney General

Subscribed and sworn to before me this fifth day of January, two thousand and fifteen.

_____

Thomas R. Lee
Associate Chief Justice, Utah Supreme Court

V's

Vermont
Virginia

State of Vermont

I, __Peter Shumlin__ , do solemnly swear that I will be true and faithful to the State of Vermont, and that I will not, directly or indirectly, do any act or thing injurious to the Constitution or Government thereof. SO HELP ME GOD.

I do solemnly swear that I will support the Constitution of the United States. SO HELP ME GOD.

I, __Peter Shumlin__ , do solemnly swear that I will faithfully execute the office of Governor for the State of Vermont and will therein do equal right and justice to all persons, to the best of my judgment and ability, according to law. SO HELP ME GOD.

_____
Peter Shumlin

STATE OF VERMONT

Washington County, ss.

At __Montpelier__ , in said County this _9th_ day of __January__ A.D., 2013 personally appeared _Peter Shumlin_ and took and subscribed the foregoing Oaths of office and allegiance.

Before me _____

2-10-15

State of Vermont

I, __Phil Scott__, do solemnly swear that I will be true and faithful to the State of Vermont, and that I will not, directly or indirectly, do any act or thing injurious to the Constitution or Government thereof. SO HELP ME GOD.

I do solemnly swear that I will support the Constitution of the United States. SO HELP ME GOD.

I, __*Phil Scott*__, do solemnly swear that I will faithfully execute the office of __Lieutenant Governor__ for the State of Vermont and will therein do equal right and justice to all persons, to the best of my judgment and ability, according to law. SO HELP ME GOD.

_____
Phil Scott

Washington County, ss.

At __Montpelier__, in said County this 6th day of __January__ A.D., 2011 personally appeared __Phil Scott__ and took and subscribed the foregoing Oaths of office and allegiance.

Before me _____

COMMONWEALTH OF VIRGINIA

OATH

_____

I do solemnly swear (or affirm) that I will support the Constitution of the United States, and the Constitution of the Commonwealth of Virginia, and that I will faithfully and impartially discharge all the duties incumbent upon me as Governor of the Commonwealth of Virginia according to the best of my ability; (so help me God).

Terence R. McAuliffe

This is to certify that Terence R. McAuliffe, on this 11th day of January, Anno Domini, 2014, took and subscribed the oath required by the laws of the Commonwealth of Virginia to qualify him to discharge the duties of Governor of the Commonwealth of Virginia.

Cynthia D. Kinser
Chief Justice
Supreme Court of Virginia

COMMONWEALTH OF VIRGINIA

OATH

_____

    I do solemnly swear (or affirm) that I will support the Constitution of the United States, and the Constitution of the Commonwealth of Virginia, and that I will faithfully and impartially discharge all the duties incumbent upon me as Lieutenant Governor of the Commonwealth of Virginia according to the best of my ability; (so help me God).

Ralph S. Northam

    This is to certify that Ralph S. Northam, on this 11th day of January, Anno Domini, 2014, took and subscribed the oath required by the laws of the Commonwealth of Virginia to qualify him to discharge the duties of Lieutenant Governor of the Commonwealth of Virginia.

Glen A. Tyler
Judge, 2nd Judicial Circuit
of Virginia, Retired

255

Office of the Secretary of the Commonwealth

OATH OF OFFICE

I do solemnly swear (or affirm) that I will support the Constitution of the United States, and the

Constitution of the Commonwealth of Virginia, and that I will faithfully and impartially discharge all of

the duties incumbent on me as

The Secretary of the Commonwealth

according to the best of my ability; (so help me God).

_____
Signature

This is to certify that   **Levar M. Stoney**

on this seventeenth day of January, 2014, took and subscribed the oath required by the laws of the

Commonwealth of Virginia to qualify him to discharge the duties as

The Secretary of the Commonwealth

_____
Justice William Mims
Virginia Supreme Court

COMMONWEALTH OF VIRGINIA

OATH

I do solemnly swear (or affirm) that I will support the Constitution of the United States, and the Constitution of the Commonwealth of Virginia, and that I will faithfully and impartially discharge all the duties incumbent upon me as Attorney General of the Commonwealth of Virginia according to the best of my ability; (so help me God).

Mark R. Herring

This is to certify that Mark R. Herring, on this 11th day of January, Anno Domini, 2014, took and subscribed the oath required by the laws of the Commonwealth of Virginia to qualify him to discharge the duties of Attorney General of the Commonwealth of Virginia.

Thomas D. Horne
*Judge, 20th Judicial Circuit
of Virginia, Retired*

257

W's

Washington
West Virginia
Wisconsin
Wyoming

OATH FOR THE OFFICE OF
GOVERNOR

I, Jay Inslee, do solemnly swear (or affirm) that I will support the constitution of the United States and the Constitution and laws of the state of Washington, and that I will faithfully discharge the duties of Governor of the State of Washington to the best of my ability.

Subscribed on this 16th day of January, 2013.

_____
Jay Inslee
Governor

Administered and Certified:

FILED

JAN 2 2 2013

SECRETARY OF STATE
STATE OF WASHINGTON

_____
Chief Justice Barbara Madsen
Chief Justice of the Supreme Court

OATH FOR THE OFFICE OF
LIEUTENANT GOVERNOR

I, Brad Owen, do solemnly swear (or affirm) that I will support the constitution of the United States and the Constitution and laws of the state of Washington, and that I will faithfully discharge the duties of Lieutenant Governor to the best of my ability.

Subscribed on this 16th day of January, 2013.

Freedom
FOREVER

Brad Owen
Lieutenant Governor

Administered and Certified:

FILED

JAN 2 2 2013

SECRETARY OF STATE
STATE OF WASHINGTON

Justice James Johnson
Justice of the Supreme Court

OATH FOR THE OFFICE OF
SECRETARY OF STATE

I, Kim Wyman, do solemnly swear (or affirm) that I will support the constitution of the United States and the Constitution and laws of the state of Washington, and that I will faithfully discharge the duties of Secretary of State to the best of my ability.

Subscribed on this 16th day of January, 2013.

_____
Kim Wyman
Secretary of State

Administered and Certified:

_____
Justice Susan Owens
Justice of the Supreme Court

RECEIVED
STATE AUDITOR
13 JAN 22 P1:2

FILED

JAN 3 1 2013

SECRETARY OF STATE
STATE OF WASHINGTON

OATH FOR THE OFFICE OF
ATTORNEY GENERAL

I, Bob Ferguson, do solemnly swear (or affirm) that I will support the constitution of the United States and the Constitution and laws of the state of Washington, that I will faithfully discharge the duties of Attorney General to the best of my ability, and that I will comply with the provisions of RCW 43.10.115.

Subscribed on this 16th day of January, 2013.

Liberty
FOREVER

_____
Bob Ferguson
Attorney General

Administered and Certified:

FILED

JAN 2 2 2013

SECRETARY OF STATE
STATE OF WASHINGTON

_____
Justice Steven González
Justice of the Supreme Court

262

OATH OF OFFICE
OF ATTORNEY GENERAL
OF WEST VIRGINIA

STATE OF WEST VIRGINIA,
COUNTY OF KANAWHA, to wit:

I, Patrick Morrisey, do solemnly swear or affirm, that I will support The Constitution of the United States of America, and the Constitution of the State of West Virginia, and that I will faithfully discharge the duties of the office of Attorney General of West Virginia, to the best of my skill and judgment, SO HELP ME GOD.

Name and Address: Patrick Morrisey
126 Rebels Roost Court
Harpers Ferry, West Virginia 25425

Signature of Affiant:

Patrick Morrisey

Honorable Patrick Morrisey

Subscribed and sworn to before me, in the County of Kanawha, State of West Virginia, this 14th day of January, 2013.

Brent Benjamin

Honorable Brent D. Benjamin
Chief Justice
Supreme Court of Appeals of West Virginia

OATH OF OFFICE AND CERTIFICATE
SEC OF STATE

STATE OF WEST VIRGINIA

COUNTY OF _Kanawha_ _____ **TO-WIT**

I, _Natalie E. Tennant_ do solemnly swear that I will support the Constitution of The United States of America and the Constitution of the State of West Virginia, and that I will faithfully discharge the duties of the office of _____ _Secretary of State_ _____ to the best of my skill and judgement SO HELP ME GOD.

Print Name and Address:
Natalie E. Tennant
849 Maple Rd.
Charleston, WV 25302

(Signature of affiant) _Natalie E. Tennant_

Subscribed and sworn to before me, in said County and State, this _14th_ day of _January_ , 20 _13_

Penny J. Barker

My Commission Expires 12/28/2022

264

30639

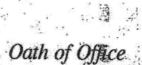

Oath of Office

State of Wisconsin)
)ss.
County of Dane   )

    I, the undersigned, who have been elected, to the office of Governor of the State of Wisconsin, but have not yet entered upon the duties thereof, swear (or affirm) that I will support the Constitution of the United States and the Constitution of the State of Wisconsin, and will faithfully discharge the duties of said office to the best of my ability. So help me God.

Scott K. Walker

Subscribed and sworn to before me this 30th day of December, 2010.

My Commission Expires: is permanent

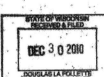

30640

Oath of Office

State of Wisconsin)
)ss:
County of Dane)

    I, the undersigned, who have been elected to the office of **Lieutenant Governor of the State of Wisconsin**, but have not yet entered upon the duties thereof, swear (or affirm) that I will support the Constitution of the United States and the Constitution of the State of Wisconsin, and will faithfully discharge the duties of said office to the best of my ability. So help me God.

Rebecca Kleefisch
Rebecca Kleefisch

Subscribed and sworn to before me
this *3 0* day of December, 2010.

Dorothy J. Marie

My Commission Expires: *3-10-2013*

OATH OF OFFICE
GOVERNOR

I do solemnly swear (or affirm) that I will support, obey and defend the constitution of the United States, and the constitution of this state; and that I will discharge the duties of my office with fidelity; that I have not paid or contributed, or promised to pay or contribute, either directly or indirectly, any money or other valuable thing, to procure my nomination or election, (or appointment) except for necessary and proper expenses expressly authorized by law; that I have not knowingly violated any election law of the state, or procured it to be done by others in my behalf; that I will not knowingly receive, directly or indirectly, any money or other valuable thing for the performance or nonperformance of any act or duty pertaining to my office, other than the compensation allowed by law.

Dated as of this 2nd day of January, 2007

David D. Freudenthal

267

OATH OF OFFICE
SECRETARY OF STATE

I do solemnly swear (or affirm) that I will support, obey, and defend the constitution of the United States, and the constitution of this state, and that I will discharge the duties of my office with fidelity; that I have not paid or contributed, or promised to pay or contribute, either directly or indirectly, any money or other valuable thing, to procure my nomination or election (or appointment) except for necessary and proper expenses expressly authorized by law; that I have not knowingly violated any election law of the state, or procured it to be done by others in my behalf; that I will not knowingly receive, directly or indirectly, any money or other valuable thing for the performance or nonperformance of any act or duty pertaining to my office, other than the compensation allowed by law.

Dated as of this 2nd day of January, 2007.

Max Maxfield

The preceding pages are examples of actual-Contracts that have been Autographed/Signed for those individuals that are in Public-Office. These contracts are also known as Federal-Contracts. The reason why these contracts are Federal is because they "swear to uphold and defend the U. S. Constitution". However, which 'Constitution' are they swearing to uphold?

The 'original' United States Constitution was written by our fore-fathers to set 'Limits' on what the Government could do against American-Civilians and was not meant for the "Subsidiaries" to-change our "Civil Rights" which is a part of the United States Constitution – a contract, into 'Privileges' and charge fees for them for their corporate-gain.

Now the House of Representatives (Congressmen and women) and The Senate (U. S. Senators) also, by law are required to Autograph/Sign the same "Contract" before they assume office. However, the Corporate-Government, the Parent-Corporation (Washington D. C.) refuses to produce any documentation in support for any of these employees. Therefore, they too are now in "BREACH OF CONTRACT" and can be held accountable for the abuse of authority and other charges.

Every President, Senator, Congressmen/women, Judges, Lawyers and Bureaucrats agree that the "Oath of Office" is a "**CONTRACT**".

We want to thank the Presidential Library in Georgia for the copy of President Jimmy Carter's (retired) for the Oath and Affirmation.

Chapter 5

THE AUTHOR'S LAST WORD

Within this book we have given and enlightened you with the golden-key that unlocks how that we, as American-Civilians, can go after the so-called U. S. Corporate-Government, Inc. professionals that claim "it is just a job". We did not realize that committing "Breach of Contract" and what is tantamount to High-Treason, Organized-Crime-Practices, Terrorist Threats, Acts of Terrorism and War-Crimes against American-Civilians was a "job" or a career.

The U. S. Corporate-Government, Inc. is not a "Democracy"; that is just an illusion to keep you into thinking and believing that you are helping by doing your "DUTY" by casting your "VOTE" during election years. The 'elected officials' and the 'bureaucrats' try to keep all FREE American-Civilians who know the difference between "privileges" and "RIGHTS" ignorant of the fact that they have 'over-all control' by what they call "Color of Law" or "Color of Jurisdiction". This belief will be the actual cause of their demise, downfall and collapse, just as Rome fell so will the U. S. Corporate Government (and it won't be a pretty sight). It is no wonder why other Countries dislike or even HATE the United States.

Washington D. C. is the actual 'Parent-Corporation' of

the fifty (50) different subsidiaries. Each State is a subsidiary of that 'Parent-Corporation'. Every Corporation has its own "POLICIES and PROCEDURES" they are not LAW. Policies and procedures are guidelines used by Corporations to make sure they operate smoothly, internally as well as externally. In addition, an individual cannot challenge a 'policy or procedure' in a court of LAW; at least that is what the courts and politicians want you to believe. Any American can challenge a LAW, but in truth if the law is making revenue for the "Corporation" then why would the courts want to change them? Even if those laws are extremely controversial (such as gun control or abortion, but we can also use Welfare as one of those concerns that's just as controversial to some concerned Americans).

First of all, when we wrote these books, Robert and I did not write them to get sympathy or use it as a "get-rich-quick-scheme" by writing about these accounts, but to 'Enlighten' you, the reader and American, as to what the real 'truth' was and still is. Granted you may be telling yourself that there is or was a 'different choice' that we could have made, but I challenge anyone to go through what we did and see if you can make those 'different-choices' for a different outcome.

But to show you, the reader that these subsidiaries "lie" through their teeth to punish those Americans that have hard-factual-proof and can prove that they are innocent or for those Americans who prove that the Corporate-Government is committing crimes or allowing other Major Companies to Commit Crimes against Americans under the guise of "That's how we do Business".

Al Capone was "doing business as well" and so was Adolph Hitler. But it did not make what they did legal... it is the same way for the 50 Subsidiaries (States Inc.) and the Parent-Corporate-Government (UNITED STATES GOVERNMENT, Inc. in Washington D. C.).

We are using our experiences from what we went

through directly, therefore no-one can claim that what we are relaying through these books as "hear-say" but facts by using their own evidence against those individuals that with Malicious Intent and Committing crimes against FREE American-Civilians.

With our particular cases that we are involved with we state facts...not opinions or lies. We also prove it by giving examples of what this Corporate-Government does illegally and calls it business. "Actions speak louder than words". In our situation, from what we went through in the Subsidiary-Corporate-State of California, we reported and exposed a major crime that was and still is being inflicted and committed against all Indigenous-Americans, American-Civilians, and U. S. Citizens alike. What followed and what the Government-Perpetrators brought against us was a "BREACH OF CONTRACT" that was tantamount to High Treason, False Accusations, Fraud upon the Court, Civil Right Violations all done with Malicious-Intent to stop us from enlightening the masses and the public of their criminal actions.

The United States-Corporate-Government, Inc. and the Judicial System rely on Ambiguities, Opinions and out-right Lies. They never want any "TRUTH" introduced into their courts as it does not generate any monies that they can legally steal from their victims. Therefore the courts HAVE to keep the "Damning Evidence that is brought against them or Elected-Officials out of their Courts" under the guise of Ambiguity, Opinion, and out-right Lies.

The so-called "jury-trial" we were forced to attend was for the benefit of taking our evidence from us and covering up the crime that we reported. We reported the crime to a number of government-entities like Congressman Sonny Bono, Mayors of the five Cities that are located in the Southern part of Coachella Valley throughout Riverside County. Congressman Sonny Bono was kind enough to send a reply when we asked for his help. He and his staff explained that "since the case is in the court system for 'Power-Theft' his office could not get involved", unfortunately this also was part of the cause of Congressman Bono's early demise. However, when we reported the crime to United States Senator barbara levy boxer (a Zionist-CUNT), now retired, with Malice, Intent and Threats to do Great Bodily Harm, through her actions and/or orders and through Abuse of Authority, her lack of attention and actions was the first "Zionist-CUNT" ("stupid/contemptible person of either gender". "An unpleasant or stupid person". In this case the term is meant only for one-individual by name in this paragraph. The definition found on google and is a viable-word used within this instance to describe the "decision and actions" that were taken against us for exposing a crime against all Americans and the World Governments in General) too be elected in the Subsidiary-Corporate-State of California, Inc. She ordered the Bureaucratic-Officials to "Put us out of our Home; Demolish our Home and get rid of us anyway they can and not necessarily in that order". The Subsidiary-Riverside-County, Inc.'s Sheriffs' Department stated to us that if we "returned to our home we would be killed". We had no choice but to leave very rapidly and try to seek help from outside of this crooked and corrupt Subsidiary-State...but to no avail. Unfortunately every time we reported the crime to the other Subsidiary-States their claim was "Oh we cannot get involved! It does not apply to us"! The crime that is being committed through the Billing-Process of all Electric Companies and it does directly apply to them and their constituents but since they refused to get involved it makes them "Accomplices" after the Fact. Therefore this is where their Elected Officials, Judges, Lawyers, and their staff-members are in "BREACH OF CONTRACT" toward the "Public".

The First-lie that County-Officials reported publically was that "we were stealing electricity for twenty-years". In truth, we started construction of our home in 1983. We had our own source for Electricity. Pictures can be found in our book "! At GUN POINT"…published in 2012. The Second-lie that County-Officials reported publically was that "we did not pay any of our 'Property-Taxes' from 1990 forward {for ten-years (10 years)}. However, yet again we tried to prove to these insidious bureaucrats through "TAX-RECIEPTS" from that County, that we still have, that we were paid up until 1997. Therefore the Bureaucrats "Falsified" Property information in writing. The Third lie that the County-Officials reported to the public was that "Our home was never there". Our home was being treated as if the Public witnessed an 'Unidentified Flying Object'. This is the sort of business that the Subsidiary-State of California conducts on a daily basis.

We were blocked at every turn, to be able to present any and all of our evidence that proves and proved our innocence and how crooked and corrupt they really were…and still are. The actions and the decisions from the United States Senator (retired) and the other perpetrators involved within this case was the basis for Malicious-Intent for "revenge" for exposing what they were trying to and continue to cover-up which in truth was Laundering of "FREE-MONEY" from the Electric Companies.

The Lie that the County 'Imposter' of the Subsidiary-Torrance County and the Magistrate reported and accused me of was "PUBLIC-DRUNK". I was separated from my witnesses and I did not have any legal-representation present at the time. What I find so amusing about this situation was that the Subsidiary-State of New Mexico does not have a law on the books about "PUBLIC DRUNK". Yet I spent 30 days in Jail for a charge that does not exist. The Subsidiary-Corporate-State of New Mexico became an accomplice after I was arrested for a charge that was not even in existence in addition to the False-accusations from an imposter who claimed to be a "Prosecutor, a State Officer, a Judge, Jury and Executioner". Yet once again, I have the evidence to show my "Innocence" of any wrongs.

After my release, I was instructed to "Get out of New Mexico or you will die!" We reported this crime to the Governor of the Subsidiary-State of New Mexico and she did nothing...yet again this is "BREACH OF CONTRACT", False-Accusations, and tantamount to HIGH TREASON, and FRAUD UPON THE COURT.

Because of the lack of help and the illegal actions taken against us, we the authors of this book, have no faith, respect, nor trust for this UNITED STATES-CORPORATE-GOVERNMENT, INC.

When and if the Politicians or Bureaucrats violate your Civil Rights they lose jurisdiction, authority and immunity under "BREACH OF CONTRACT". This is not an opinion, but a fact that passed lawmakers placed into law.

Please Note: This author will NOT redact, retract nor offer any apologies for the terminology within this chapter or book. If you readers are offended...so be it. As it was stated to me a number of times "GET OVER IT". In addition, if the retired senator of Ca. tries to make the above terminology into a legal-matter under Slander and Defamation...try. I have all the evidence and witnesses that I speak the truth through the facts that were and have been presented for us and you will be exposed for what you really are. The same goes for the Subsidiary-State of New Mexico and its perpetrators.

We may not be wealthy money-wise, but we have something they do not have...HONOR, INTEGRITY, CREDIBILITY and THE TRUTH!

A **writ** is a document that is written and is signed/ autographed and then Notarized by a Notary-Public, with other witnesses.

A **Declaration** is a document that is written out and witnessed by at least six (6) witnesses (which tantamount to being a Petite-Jury) and with your signature/autograph attached-thereto. In other words Sign/Autograph the document...this document does not need to be notarized.

The following is a **"PUBLIC-ANNOUNCEMENT"** for all those Subsidiary-Corporate-Governments, Inc. (all 50 of them) that with the belief that all American-Civilians are a Corporation, Incorporated or are made into Businesses and are forced into participating in their form of "Organized-Crime-Practices" that forces the American-Civilian to pay FEES, PENALTIES or FINES.

DECLARATION OF INTENTIONS:

I, Bradley – Jefferson: [Franks], an American live-born-individual, hereby: **rescind, reject, revoke, cancel, suspend-indefinitely** any and all Federal/**Federal INC.**; Federal-State/**State INC.**; County/**County INC.**; City/**City INC.**; "contracts" that they believe they have over-my individual-live-personage.

I, Bradley – Jefferson: [Franks] also hereby, **rescind, revoke, cancel, and suspend-indefinitely** any and **ALL** Signatures/Autographs affixed on any "Contracts" that have been produced by said above-perpetrators for the reasons of "lack of Full-Disclosure" this includes and is not limited to **"Implied Contracts"**.

As an American-Civilian, I, Bradley – Jefferson: [Franks] have the RIGHT (by the "CONSTITUTION") for any contract for my **"LIFE, LIBERTY, and PURSUIT OF HAPPINESS"** without interference, negligence, force, coercion, blackmail, threats or any other Organized-Criminal Practices brought-against or applied-against me through what the Government, Inc. calls "license, permits or fees".

Any deviation of this "Public-Announcement" from any FEDERAL, Inc., STATE, Inc., COUNTY, Inc. or CITY, Inc. ADMINISTRATION will be considered an **ACT OF WAR** and will be subject to Penalties and Fines for "**BREACH OF CONTRACT**" under the guise of "DOING-BUSINESS" through their "**Franchise-Tax-Boards**".

All of the above is **TRUE** and **CORRECT**! So help me **GOD**!

By my-own electronic-autograph: Bradley - Jefferson: [Franks];

Date: February 12, 2018.

For those readers who want to get out of the Yoke of Slavery, being-Indentured, or having to comply with the United-State-Corporate-Government, Inc. use this document for your intentions. You can make changes as necessary that suits your individual-needs.

We are not writing this book to enlighten those who choose to turn a blind-eye and a deaf-ear to those who need help. We are writing this book to educate those Countries that need information that will "PUNISH" the United States-Corporate-Government, Inc. for "BREACH OF CONTRACT" and "WAR CRIMES".

We have added a Glossary for those who do not have a Black's Law Dictionary or access to one for your convenience only and for the definitions for some of the terminology within this book.

Chapter 6

GLOSSARY OF TERMINOLOGY
AND DEFINITIONS

"**Law and Motion Waltz**": To help in the definition of the "Law and Motion Calendar" aka "Law and Motion Waltz" is actually on the basis that the "games" that are played in the discovery-phase result in what is deemed a "Game of Kings". If you are trying to represent yourself as your own counsel/attorney you are called a "Pro Se Litigant". Unfortunately you start-off at a disadvantage on the basis that you are not a "State-Bar [Licensed] Attorney". (However, remember "Counsels/Attorneys" do not have a "State-License" either).

As a Pro Se Litigant you are defenseless against the "school of sharks". Furthermore, there are many technicalities that can defeat you if you are not properly prepared with the groundwork that helps "Establish a Cause of Action" as is defined in "Tort Law"; the key is to bring "Facts in Evidence" that will lead you for a Cause of Action. The "Rules" for a Pro Se Litigant are different from a "Counsel/Attorney of Record". However if you are able to avoid the "Pitfalls of Pro Se Litigation" your Cause of Action will not be easily denied. The first thing you have to do is to "break-down" each Cause of Action into its simplest form of "Principles". By attacking the "Gravamen of the Complaint", you make your stand and proceed in a manner that you can explain your case to a five-year-old; making the case so-simple that no-judge can dismiss your case on the basis that they "do not understand what you are saying." (even though we speak Plain-English).

The heart of properly playing the "Law and Motion-game" is to stay-alive by properly using the "Meet and Confer Letter" as a means of filling in the gaps that may be used against you in a surprise-attack in open-court by properly "Preparing for a Hearing". Do not leave any gaps that can cause your opponent to make a surprise attack. You have to make them "jump-over-the-fence", on "record", in "open court" to make their attack. If you have properly established-a-Cause of Action, the fence is usually set a lot higher and may deter them from making a surprise attack.

I you properly admit your "Facts in Evidence", the opposing party will most likely want to settle the case if they are not successful in a "Demurrer"; furthermore, they will be forced to provide you with a settlement to make the case go away. However, most Pro Se Litigants are dismissed "Without Prejudice" (which is laughable – because they really are "prejudiced") and therefore cause a "cloud" over their "Cause of Action" that is intended to deter them from attempting to bring the matter before the court again on the basis of "Estoppel". In the long run, by avoiding the "Pitfalls of Pro Se Litigation" you are forcing a settlement agreement in your favor. Furthermore, by properly playing the "Law and Motion Waltz" you will remain level with the court.

The reality of this matter is that a "Pro Se Litigant" does not burn-through monetary-resources as you would with a high-priced "Counsel/Attorney". If you are able to maintain your position and cause, survive a "Motion for Summary Judgement" and/or a "Demurrer", you will become a part of a select few that will be allowed on the "Dance-floor with the Kings in the Waltz" that will allow you to proceed. If you maintain you focus, avoid the Pitfalls of the Pro Se Litigants, you may very well find a very good settlement in your favor. The key is to keep a strong defensive-strategy and keep your area safe from attack. The opposing side will have to find a favorable settlement because the alternative will ultimately result in an unfavorable judgement against them. In addition, without a Counsel/Attorney bleeding your scarce financial resources dry, you have the ability to fight another day until your matter is heard.

Allegation: the assertion, claim, declaration, or statement of a party to an action, made in a pleading, setting out what he expects to prove.

Appeal: the resort to a superior court to review the decision of an inferior court or administrative agency. A complaint to a higher tribunal of an error or injustice committed by a lower tribunal, in which the error or injustice is sought to be corrected or reversed.

Artifice: An ingenious contrivance or device of some kind, and, when used in a bad sense, it corresponds with trick or fraud. It implies craftiness and deceit and imports some element of moral obliquity.

Attorney-Client Privilege: In law of evidence, client's privilege to refuse to disclose and to prevent any other person from disclosing confidential communications between him and his attorney. Such privilege protects communications between attorney and client made for purpose of furnishing or obtaining professional legal advice or assistance.

Attorney of Record: Attorney whose name must appear somewhere in permanent records or files of case, or on the pleadings or some instrument filed in the case, or on appearance docket.

Person whom the client has named as his agent upon whom service of papers may be made.

An attorney who has filed a notice of appearance and who hence is formally mentioned in court records as the official attorney of the party. Once an attorney becomes an attorney of record, he often cannot withdraw from the case without court permission.

Every pleading of a party represented by an attorney shall be signed by at least one attorney of record in his individual name, whose address shall be stated.

Bill: As a legal term, this word has many meanings and applications, the most important are set forth within this Glossary for your benefit for your case and evidence against those under "Breach of Contract".

Bill of attainder: Legislative acts, no matter what their form, that apply either to named individuals or to easily ascertainable members of a group in such a way as to inflict punishment on them without a judicial trial. An act is a "bill of attainder" when the punishment is death and a "bill of pains and penalties" when the punishment is less severe; both kinds of punishment fall within the scope of the constitutional prohibition. U. S. Constitution; Article I: Section: 9, Clause: 3 (as to Congress); Article I: Section: 10 (as to state legislatures).

Bill of Rights: A formal and emphatic legislative assertion and declaration of popular rights and liberties- (NOT PRIVELEDGES for the payment of: emphasis added)-usually promulgated upon a change of government; e. g. the famous Bill of Rights of 1688 in English history. Also the summary of the rights and liberties of the people, or of the principles of constitutional law deemed essential and fundamental, contained in many of the American state constitutions. That portion of Constitution guaranteeing "rights" and "liberties" (NOT PRIVELEDGES – emphasis added) to the individual; i. e. first ten Amendments of the United States of America Constitution. (This is a CONTRACT – emphasis added).

Blood Money: A wergild, or pecuniary mulct paid by a slayer to the relatives of his victims. Also used, in a popular sense, as descriptive of money paid by way of reward for the apprehension and conviction of a person charged with a capital crime.

Breach: The breaking or violating of a law, right, obligation, engagement, or duty, either by commission or omission. Exists where one party to contract fails to carry out term, promise, or condition of the contract.

Breach of Contract: Failure, without legal excuse, to perform any promise which forms the whole or part of a contract. Prevention or hindrance by party to contract of any occurrence or performance requisite under the contract for the creation or continuation of a right in favor of the other party or the discharge of a duty by him. Unequivocal, distinct and absolute refusal to perform agreement.

Cause of Action: The facts or facts which give a person a right to judicial redress or relief against another. The legal effect of an occurrence in terms of redress to a party to the occurrence. A situation or state of facts which would entitle party to sustain action and give him right to seek a judicial remedy in his behalf. Fact or a state of facts, to which law sought to be enforced against a person or thing applies. Facts which give rise to one or more relations of right-duty between two or more persons. Failure to perform legal obligation to do, or refrain from performance of, some act. Matter for which action may be maintained. Unlawful violation or invasion of right. The right which a party has to institute a judicial proceeding.

Circumstantial Evidence: Testimony not based on actual personal knowledge or observation of the facts from which deductions are drawn, showing indirectly the facts sought to be proved. The proof of certain facts and circumstances in a given case, from which jury may infer other connected facts which usually and reasonably follow according to the common experience of mankind. Evidence of facts or circumstances from which the existence or nonexistence of fact in issue may be inferred. Inferences drawn from facts proved. Process of decision by which court or jury may reason from circumstances known or proved, to establish by inference the principle fact. It means that existence of principle facts is only inferred from circumstances.

The proof of various facts or circumstances which usually attend the main fact in dispute, and therefore tend to prove its existence, or to sustain, by their consistency, the hypothesis claimed. Or as otherwise defined, it consists in reasoning from facts which are known or proved to establish such as are conjectured to exist.

Class or representative action: A class action provides a means by which, where a large group of persons are interested in a matter, one or more may sue or be sued as representatives of the class without needing to join every member of the class. This procedure is available in federal court and in most state courts under Rule of Civil Procedure 23.

There are general requirements for the maintenance of any class suit. These are that the persons constituting the class must be so numerous that it is impracticable to bring them all before the court, and the named representatives must be such as will fairly insure the adequate representation of them all. In addition, there must be an ascertainable class and there must be a well-defined common interest in the questions of law and fact involved affecting the parties to be represented. The trial court must also certify the lawsuit as a class action.

Prior to the revision of Federal Civil Procedure Rule 23 in 1966, there were three categories of class actions, popularly known as "true", "hybrid", and "spurious". These categories no longer exist under present Rule 23.

Coercion: Compulsion; constraint; compelling by force or arms or threat. It may be actual, direct, or positive, as where physical force is used to compel act against one's will, or implied, legal or constructive, as where one party is constrained by subjugation to other to do what his free will would refuse. As used in testamentary law, any pressure by which testator's action is restrained against his free will in the execution of his testament. "Coercion" that vitiates confession can be mental as well as physical, and question is whether accused was deprived of his free choice to admit, deny, or refuse to answer.

A person is guilty of criminal coercion if, with purpose to unlawfully restrict another's freedom of action to his detriment, he threatens to: (a) commit any criminal offense; or (b) accuse anyone of a criminal offense; or (c) expose any secret tending to subject any person to hatred, contempt or ridicule, or to impair his credit or business repute; or (d) take or withhold action as an official, or cause an official to take or withhold action. Model Penal Code: §: 212.5.

Collusion: An agreement between two or more persons to defraud a person of his rights by the forms of law, or to obtain an object forbidden by law. It implies the existence of fraud of some kind, the employment of fraudulent means, or of lawful means for the accomplishment of an unlawful purpose. A secrete combination, conspiracy, or concert of action between two or more persons for fraudulent or deceitful purpose.

Colore officii: Latin. By color of office. Officer's acts unauthorized by officer's position, though done in form that purports that acts are done by reason of official duty and by virtue of office.

Color of authority: That semblance or presumption of authority sustaining the acts of a public officer which is derived from his apparent title to the office or from a writ or other purpose in his hands apparently valid and regular.

Color of law: The appearance or semblance, without the substance, of legal right. Misuse of power, possessed by virtue of state law and made possible only because wrongdoer is clothed with authority of state, is action taken under "color of state law".

When used in the context of federal civil rights statutes or criminal law, the term is synonymous with the concept of "state action" under the Fourteenth Amendment, and means pretense of law and includes actions of officers who undertake to perform their official duties.

Action taken by private individuals may be "under color of state law" for purposes of Title: 42; United State Codes Annotated: § 1983; governing deprivation of civil rights when significant state involvement attaches to action.

Acts "under color of law" of a State include not only acts done by State officials within the bounds or limits of their lawful authority, but also acts done without and beyond the bounds of their lawful authority; provided that, in order for unlawful acts of an official to be done "under any color of any law", the unlawful acts must be done while such official is purporting or pretending to act in the performance of his official duties; that is to say the unlawful acts must consist in an abuse or misuse of power which is possessed by the official only because he is an official; and the unlawful acts must be of such a nature or character, and be committed under such circumstances, that they would not have occurred but for the fact that the person committing them was an official then and there exercising his official powers outside the bounds of lawful authority. "Title: 42; United States Codes Annotated: § 1983".

Color of office: Pretense of official right to do act made by one who has no such right. An act under color of office is an act of an officer who claims authority to do the act by reason of his office when the office does not confer on him any such authority.

Conclusive Presumptions: Exists when an ultimate fact is presumed to be true upon proof of another fact, and no evidence, no matter how persuasive, can rebut it; an example is the presumption that a child less than a specified age is unable to consent to sexual intercourse.

Constitution: The organic and fundamental law of a nation or state, which may be written or unwritten, establishing the character and conception of its government, laying the basic principles to which its internal life is conformed, organizing the (corporate – emphasis added) government, and regulating, distributing, and limiting the functions of its different departments, and prescribing the extent and manner of the exercise of sovereign powers. A charter of government deriving its whole authority from the governed (emphasis added). The written instrument agreed upon by the people of the Union (e. g. United State of America Constitution) or of a particular state, as the absolute rule of action and decision for all departments (i. e. branches) and officers of the government in respect to all the points covered by it, which must control until it shall be changed by the authority which established it (i. e. by amendment), and in opposition to which any act or ordinance of ant such department or officer is null and void. (The Constitution is a contract that limits government in its actions against Americans. Furthermore, the first Ten Amendments are part of this Contract – emphasis added).

Contract: An agreement between two or more persons which creates an obligation to do or not to do a particular thing. As defined in Restatement, Second, Contracts § 3: "A contract is a promise or a set of promises for the breach of which the law gives a remedy, or the performance of which the law in some way recognizes as a duty". A legal relationship consisting of the rights and duties of the contracting parties; a promise or set of promises constituting an agreement between the parties that gives each a legal duty to the other and also the right to seek a remedy for the breach of those duties. Its essentials are competent parties, subject matter, a legal consideration, mutuality of agreement, and mutuality of obligation.

Under U.C.C., term refers to total legal obligation which results from parties' agreement as affected by the Code. Section 1-201(11). As to sales, "contract" and "agreement" are limited to those relating to present or future sales of goods, and "contract for sale" includes both a present sale of goods and a contract to sell goods at a future time. U.C.C. § 2-106(1).

The writing which contains the agreement of parties, with the terms and conditions, and which serves as a proof of the obligation.

Contracts may be classified on several different methods, according to the element in them which is brought into prominence. The usual classifications are as follows: Blanket contract, Certain and Hazardous, Commutative and independent, Conditional contract, Consensual and real, Constructive contract, Cost-Plus contract, Divisible and indivisible, Entire and severable, Entire contract clause, Exclusive contract, Executed and executory, Express and implied, Gratuitous and onerous, Investment contract, Joint and several, Mutual interest, mixed, etc., Open end contract, Output contract, Parol contract, Personal contract, Pre-contract, Principal and accessory contract, Quasi contract, Record, specialty, simple contracts, Requirements contract, Shipment contracts, Special contract, Subcontract, Tying contract, Unconscionable contract, Unenforceable contract, Unilateral and bilateral, Usurious contract, Voidable contract, Void contract, Written Contract...Note: these are just some of the contracts, to name a few that we as Americans are forced upon voluntarily or involuntarily.

Controversy: A litigated question; adversary proceeding in a court of law; a civil action or suit, either at law or in equity; a justiciable dispute. To be a "Controversy" under federal constitutional provision limiting exercise of judicial power of the United States to cases and controversies there must be a concrete case admitting of an immediate and definitive determination of legal rights of parties in an adversary proceeding upon facts alleged, and claims based merely upon assumed potential invasions of rights are not enough to warrant judicial intervention. In the constitutional sense, it means more than a disagreement and conflict; rather it means a kind of controversy courts traditionally resolve. This term is important in that judicial power of the courts extends only to cases and "controversies".

Credibility: Worthiness of belief; that quality in a witness which renders his evidence worthy of belief. After the competence of a witness is allowed, the consideration of his credibility arises, and not before. There is a distinction between competency, credibility and reputation.

Deceit: A fraudulent and deceptive misrepresentation, artifice, or device, used by one or more persons to deceive and trick another, who is ignorant of the true facts, to the prejudice and damage of the party imposed upon. To constitute "deceit", the statement must be untrue, made with knowledge of it falsity or with reckless and conscious ignorance thereof, especially parties are not on equal terms, made with intent that plaintiff act thereon or in a manner apparently fitted to induce him to act thereon, and plaintiff must act in reliance on the statement in the manner contemplated or manifestly probable, to his injury.

Declaratory Judgement: A Statutory remedy for the determination of a justiciable controversy where the plaintiff is in doubt as to his legal rights. A binding adjudication of the rights and status of litigants even though no consequential relief is awarded. Such judgement is conclusive in a subsequent action between the parties as to the matters declared and, in accordance with the usual rules of issue preclusion, as to any issues actually litigated and determined.

Defamation: An intentional false communication, either published or publicly spoken, that injures another's reputation or good name. Holding up of a person to ridicule, scorn or contempt in a respectable and considerable part of the community; may be criminal as well as civil. Includes both libel and slander.

Defamation is that which tends to injure reputation; to diminish the esteem, respect, goodwill, or confidence in which the plaintiff is held, or to excite adverse, derogatory or unpleasant feelings or opinions against him. Statement which exposes person to contempt, hatred, ridicule, or obloquy.

The unprivileged publication of false statements which naturally and proximately result in injury to another.

To recover against a public official or public figure, plaintiff must prove that the defamatory statement was published with malice. Malice as used in this context means that it was published either knowing that it was false or with a reckless disregard as to whether it was true or false.

A communication is defamatory if it tends so to harm the reputation of another as to lower him in the estimation of the community or to deter third persons from associating or dealing with him. The meaning of a communication is that which the recipient correctly, or mistakenly but reasonably, understands that it was intended to express.

Demurrer: An allegation of a defendant, which, admitting the matters of fact alleged by complaint or bill (equity action) to be true, shows that as they are therein set forth they are insufficient for the plaintiff to proceed upon or to oblige the defendant to answer; or that, for some reason apparent on the face of the complaint or bill, or on account of the omission of some matter which ought to be contained therein, or for want of some circumstances which ought to be attendant thereon, the defendant ought not to be compelled to answer. The formal mode of disputing the sufficiency in law of the pleading of the other side. In effect it is an allegation that, even if the facts as stated in the pleading to which objection is taken be true, yet their legal consequences are not as such as to put the demurring party to the necessity of answering them or proceeding further with the cause. An assertion that complaint does not set forth a cause of action upon which relief can be granted, and it admits, for purpose of testing sufficiency of complaint, all properly pleaded facts, but not conclusions of law. A legal objection to the sufficiency of a pleading, attacking what appears on the face of the document.

By Federal Rules of Civil Procedure demurrers, pleas and exceptions for insufficiency of a pleading are abolished. Rule 7(c). Every defense in law shall be made by motion or by answer; motions going to jurisdiction, venue, process, or failure to state a claim are to be disposed of before trial, unless the court orders otherwise. While the Federal Rules do not provide for the use of a demurrer, an equivalent to a general demurrer is provided in the motion to dismiss for failure to state a claim on which relief may be granted. Federal Rules of Civil Procedure 12(b). Objections to the pleadings by means of a demurrer still exist however in certain states.

Duress: Any unlawful threat of coercion used by a person to induce another to act (or refrain from acting) in a manner he or she otherwise would not (or would). Subjecting person to improper pressure which overcomes his will and coerces him to comply with demand to which he would not yield if acting as free agent. Application of such pressure or constraint as compels man to go against his will, and takes away his free agency, destroying power of refusing to comply with unjust demands of another.

A condition where one is induced by wrongful act or threat of another to make a contract or perform a tortious act under circumstances which deprive him of exercise of his free will. Includes any conduct which overpowers will and coerces or constrains performance of an act which otherwise would not have been performed.

Duress may be a defense to a criminal act, breach of contract, or tort because an act to be criminal or one which constitutes a breach of contract or a tort must be voluntary to create liability or responsibility.

A contract entered into under duress by physical compulsion is void. Also, if a party's manifestation of assent to a contract is induced by an improper threat by the other party that leaves the victim no reasonable alternative, the contract is voidable by the victim. Restatement, Second, Contracts §§: 174, 175.

As a defense to a civil action, it must be pleaded affirmatively. Federal Rules of Civil Procedure 8 (c).

A an affirmative defense in criminal law, one who, under the pressure of an unlawful threat from another human being to harm him (or to harm a third person), commits what would otherwise be a crime may, under some circumstances, be justified in doing what he did and thus not be guilty of the crime in question. Model Penal Code §: 2.09.

Duress of imprisonment: The wrongful imprisonment of a person, or the illegal restraint of his liberty, in order to compel him to do some act.

Duressor: One who subjects another to duress; one who compels another to do a thing, as by menace.

Duress per minas: Duress by threats. The use of threats and menaces to compel a person, by the fear of death, or grievous bodily harm, as mayhem or loss of limb, to do some lawful act, or to commit a misdemeanor.

Embezzlement: The fraudulent appropriation to property by one lawfully entrusted with its possession. To "embezzle" means willfully to take, or convert to one's own use, another's money or property, of which the wrongdoer acquired possession lawfully, by reason of some office or employment or position of trust. The elements of "offense" are that there must be relationship such as that of the money and the defendant, the money alleged to have been embezzled must have come into the possession of defendant by virtue of that relationship and there must be an intentional and fraudulent appropriation or conversion of the money. The fraudulent conversion of the property of another by one who has lawful possession of the property and whose fraudulent conversion has been made punishable by statute.

Errors and Omissions: n. Shorthand for malpractice insurance which gives physicians, attorneys, architects, accountants, and other professionals coverage for claims by patients and clients for alleged professional errors and omissions which amount to negligence.

Estoppel: "Estoppel" means that party is prevented by his own acts from claiming a right to detriment of other party who was entitled to rely on such conduct and has acted accordingly. A principle that provides that an individual is barred from denying or alleging a certain fact or state facts because of that individual's previous conduct, allegation, or denial. A doctrine which holds that an inconsistent position, attitude or course of conduct may not be adopted to loss or injury of another.

Estoppel is or may be based on acceptance of benefits, actual or constructive fraudulent conduct, admissions or denials by which another is induced to act to his injury, agreement on and settlement of facts by force of entering into contract, assertion of facts on which another relies; assumption of position which, if not maintained, would result in injustice to another; concealment of facts; conduct or acts amounting to a representation or a concealment; consent to copyright infringement, whether express or implied from long acquiescence with knowledge of the infringement; election between rights or remedies, laches; language or conduct which has induced another to act.

Estoppels at common law are sometimes said to be of three kinds: (1) by deed; (2) by matter of record; (3) by matter in pais. The first two are also called legal estoppels, as distinguished from the last kind, known as equitable estoppels.

Evidence Codes: Statutory provisions governing admissibility of evidence and burden of proof at hearings and trials.

Excusable Neglect: In practice, and particularly with reference to the setting aside of a judgement taken against a party through his "excusable neglect", this means a failure to take the proper steps at the proper time, not in consequence of the party's own carelessness, in attention, or willful disregard of the process of the court, but in consequence of some unexpected or unavoidable hindrance or accident, or reliance on the care and vigilance of his counsel or on promises made by the adverse party. As used in rule: (Federal Rules of Civil Procedure 6(b)) authorizing court to permit an act to be done after expiration of the time within which under the rules such act was required to be done, where failure to act was the result of "excusable neglect", quoted phrase is ordinarily understood to be the act of a reasonably prudent person under the same circumstances. For purposes of motion to vacate judgement, "excusable neglect" is that neglect which might have been the act of a reasonably prudent person under the circumstances.

Ex parte: On one side only; by or for one party; done for, in behalf of or on application of, one party only.

A judicial proceeding, order, injunction, etc., is said to be ex parte when it is taken or granted at the instance and for the benefit of one party only, and without notice to, or contestation by, any person adversely interested.

"Ex parte", in the heading of a reported case, signifies that the name following is that of the party upon whose application the case is heard.

Facts in Evidence: included in the evidence already adduces. The "Facts in evidence" are such as have already been proven within the cause.

Factual and Procedural History: The Factual and Procedural History are used to establish your Cause of

Action. The Petition or Response should include a statement that a separate Factual and Procedural History shall be filed to substantiate the Cause of Action. This is "Establishing a Cause of Action".

Response or Petition – Pro Se Litigants are encouraged to provide a Petition or Response that merely state the Cause of Action and the Prayer for Relief. If you attempt to bury the "court" with a "lengthy dissertation" it will most likely "confuse the court" as opposed to "clearly define" your "Cause of Action". In the beginning phase of the summons and response, the court is merely seeking to understand the "Cause of Action" by each party. Generally speaking the Petition and Response have Material Facts and Allegations that are assumed to be true for the purpose of setting the matter for the ""Law and Motion Waltz" [a.k.a. Law and Motion Calendar]". Furthermore, the Petition and Response should merely provide the overview with enough detail to meet the statutory requirements that relate to your "Cause of Action".

Supporting the Petition or Response – By separating the detailed documents from the petition, the court will see a very concise statement of the matters that are intended to be brought to Trial. The court assumes that the parties will discuss the matter through the "Law and Motion Waltz" [a.k.a. Law and Motion Calendar]. The opposing side uses Law (which in truth becomes a misrepresentation of the material facts) which is intended to deceive another, does actually deceive another, and which causes harm to the one deceived. The law allows punitive damages through Motions.

Fraud: An intentional perversion of truth for the purpose of inducing another in reliance upon it to part with some valuable thing belonging to him or to surrender a legal right. A false representation of a matter of fact, whether by words or by conduct, by false or misleading allegations, or by concealment of that which should have been disclosed, which deceives and is intended to deceive another so that he shall act upon it to his legal injury. Anything calculated to deceive, whether by a single act or combination, or by suppression of truth, or suggestion of what is false, whether it be direct falsehood or innuendo, by speech or silence, word of mouth, or look or gesture. A generic term, embracing all multifarious means which human ingenuity can devise, and which are resorted to by one individual to get advantage over another by false suggestions or by suppression of truth, and includes all surprise, trick, cunning, dissembling, and any unfair way by which another is cheated. "Bad faith" and "fraud" are synonymous, and also synonyms of dishonesty, infidelity, faithlessness, perfidy, unfairness, etc.

Elements of a cause of a cause of action for "fraud" include false representation of a present or past fact made by defendant, action in reliance thereupon by plaintiff, and damage resulting to plaintiff from such misrepresentation.

As distinguished from negligence, it is always positive, intentional. It comprises all acts, omissions, and concealments involving a breach of a legal or equitable duty and resulting in damage to another. And includes anything calculated to deceive, whether it be a single act or combination of circumstances, whether the suppression of truth or the suggestion of what is false, whether it be direct falsehood or by innuendo, by speech or by silence, by word of mouth, or by look or gesture. Fraud, as applied to contracts, is the cause of an error bearing on a material part of the contract, created or continued by artifice, with design to obtain some unjust advantage to the one party, or to cause an inconvenience or loss to the other.

Extrinsic Fraud: Fraud which is collateral to the issues tried in a case where the judgement is rendered. Type of deceit which may form basis for setting aside a judgement as for example a divorce granted ex parte because the plaintiff-spouse falsely tells the court he or she is ignorant of the whereabouts of the defendant-spouse.

Fraud on Court: A scheme to interfere with judicial machinery performing task of impartial adjudication, as by preventing opposing party from fairly presenting his case or defense. Finding of fraud on the court is justified only by most egregious misconduct directed to the court itself such as bribery of a judge or jury to fabrication of evidence by counsel and must be supported by clear, unequivocal and convincing evidence. It consists of conduct so egregious that it undermines the integrity of the judicial process.

Gravamen: The material part of a grievance, complaint, indictment, charge, cause of action, etc. The Burden or gist of a charge; the grievance or injury special complained of.

Impersonation: False impersonation is representing oneself to be a public officer or employee or a person licensed to practice or engage in any profession or vocation for which a license is required by state law with knowledge that such representation is false. The act of pretending or representing oneself to be another, commonly a crime if the other is a public official or police officer.

In Propria persona: aka. "In pro per". In one's own proper person. It was formerly a rule in a pleading that pleas to the jurisdiction of the court must plead in Propria persona, because if pleaded by attorney they admit the jurisdiction, as an attorney is an officer of the court, and he is presumed to plead after obtaining leave, which admits the jurisdiction.

In rem: A technical term used to designate proceedings or actions instituted against the thing, in contradistinction to personal actions, which are said to be in personam.

"In rem" proceedings encompass any action brought against person in which essential purpose of suit is to determine title or to affect interests in specific property located within territory over which court has jurisdiction. It is true that, in a strict sense, a proceeding in rem is one taken directly against property, without reference to the title of individual claimants; but, in a larger and more general sense, the terms are applied to actions between parties, where the direct object is to reach and dispose of property owned by them, or of some interest there in. Such are cases commenced by attachment against the property of debtors, or instituted to partition real estate, foreclosure a mortgage, or enforce a lien. In the strict sense of the term, a proceeding "in rem" is one which is taken directly against property or one which is brought to enforce a right in the thing itself.

Actions in which the court is required to have control of the thing or object and in which an adjudication is made as to the object which binds the whole world and not simply the interests of the parties to the proceeding.

Intentional Fraud: A misrepresentation of a material fact which is intended to deceive another, does actually deceive another, and which causes harm to the one deceived. The Law allows punitive damages.

Jurisdiction: A term of comprehensive import embracing every kind of judicial action. It is the power of the court to decide a matter in controversy and presupposes the existence of a duly constituted court with control over the subject matter and the parties. Jurisdiction defines the powers of courts to inquire into facts, apply the law, make decisions, and declare judgement. The legal right by which judges exercise their authority. It exists when court has cognizance of class of cases involved, proper parties are present, and point to be decided is within powers of court. Power and authority of a court to hear and determine a judicial proceeding; and power to render particular judgement in question. The right and power of a court to adjudicate concerning the subject matter in a given case. The term may have different meanings in different contexts. Areas of authority; the geographic area in which a court has power or types of cases it has power to hear. Scope and extent of jurisdiction of federal courts is governed by Title: 28; United States Codes Annotated; §: 1251 et seq.

Malice: The intentional doing of a wrongful act without just cause or excuse, with an intent to inflict an injury or under circumstances that the law will imply an evil intent. A condition of mind which prompts a person to do a wrongful act willfully, that is, on purpose, to the injury of another, or to do intentionally a wrongful act toward another without justification or excuse. A conscious violation of the law (or the prompting of the mind to commit it) which operates to the prejudice of another person. A condition of the mind showing a heart regardless of social duty and fatally bent on mischief. Malice in law is not necessarily personal hate or ill will, but it is that state of mind which is reckless of law and of the legal rights of the citizen.

Malice in Fact: Express or actual malice. Ill will towards a particular person; an actual intention to injure or defame such person. It implies desire or intent to injure, while "Malice in Law", or "Implied Malice", means wrongful act done intentionally, without just cause or excuse, and jury may infer it.

Malice in law: the intentional doing of a wrongful act without just cause or excuse. Implied, inferred, or legal malice. As distinguished from malice in fact, it is presumed from tortious acts, deliberately done without just cause, excuse, or justification, which are reasonably calculated to injure another or others.

Malicious Injury: An injury committed against a person at the prompting of malice or hatred towards him, or done spitefully or wantonly. The willful doing of an act with knowledge it is liable to injure another and regardless of consequences. Injury involving element of fraud, violence, wantonness, and willfulness, or criminality. An injury that is intentional, wrongful and without just cause or excuse, even in the absence of hatred, spite or ill will. Punitive damages may be awarded to plaintiff for such injury.

Malicious Prosecution: One begun in malice without probable cause to believe the charges can be sustained.

An action for damages brought by person, against whom civil suit or criminal prosecution has been instated maliciously and without probable cause, after termination of prosecution of such suit in favor of person claiming damages.

One who takes an active part in the initiation, continuation or procurement of civil proceedings against another is subject to liability to the other for wrongful civil proceedings if: (a) he acts without probable cause, and primarily for a purpose other than that of securing the proper adjudication of the claim in which the proceedings are based, and (b) except when they are ex parte, the proceedings have terminated in favor of the person against whom they are brought. Torts, § 674.

Elements of a cause of action for malicious prosecution are: (1) commencement of prosecution of proceedings against present plaintiff; (2) its legal causation by present defendant; (3) its termination in favor of present plaintiff; (4) absence of probable cause for such proceedings; (5) presence of malice therein; and (6) damage to plaintiff by reason thereof.

In addition to the tort remedy for malicious criminal proceedings, the majority of states also permit tort actions for malicious institution of civil actions.

Malicious use of process: Utilization of process to intimidate, oppress or punish a person against whom it is sued out.

Exists where plaintiff proceeds maliciously and without probable cause to execute object which law intends process to subserve. It has to with the wrongful initiation of such process, while "abuse of civil process" is concerned with perversion of a process after it is issued.

Malitia est acida; est mali animi affectus: "Malice is sour; it is the quality of a bad mind".

Malpractice: Professional misconduct or unreasonable lack of skill. This term is usually applied to such conduct by doctors, lawyers and accountants. Failure of one rendering professional services to exercise that degree of skill and learning commonly applied under all the circumstances in the community by the average prudent reputable member of the profession with the result of injury, loss or damage to the recipient of those services or to those entitled to rely upon them. It is any professional misconduct, unreasonable lack of skill or fidelity in professional or fiduciary duties, evil practice, or illegal or immoral conduct.

Legal Malpractice: Consists of failure of an attorney to use such skill, prudence, and diligence as lawyers of ordinary skill and capacity commonly possess and exercise in performance of tasks which they undertake, and when such failure proximately causes damage it gives rise to an action in tort.

Malum non habet efficientem, sed deficientem, causam: "Evil has not an efficient, but a deficient, cause".

Material Evidence: That quality of evidence which tends to influence the trier of fact because of its logical connection with the issue. Evidence which has an effective influence or bearing on question in issue.

"Materiality" of evidence refers to pertinency of the offered evidence to the issue in dispute.

Evidence which is material to question in controversy, and which must necessarily enter into consideration of the controversy, and which by itself or in connection with other evidence is determinative of the case.

To establish Brady violation requiring reversal of a conviction, defendant must show that prosecution has suppressed evidence, that such evidence was favorable to defendant or was exculpatory, and that evidence was material; evidence is "material" if there is reasonable probability that, but for failure to produce such evidence, outcome of case would have been different.

Material Fact: Contracts. One which constitutes

substantially the consideration of the contract, or without which it would not have been made.

Pleading and Practice: One which is essential to the case, defense, application, etc., and without which it could not be supported. One which tends to establish any of issues raised. The "material facts" of an issue of fact are such as are necessary to determine the issue. Material fact is one upon which outcome of litigation depends.

Material representation or misrepresentation: A misrepresentation is "material" if it relates to a matter upon which plaintiff could be expected to rely in determining to engage in the conduct in question. In law of deceit, a statement or undertaking of sufficient substance and importance as to be the foundation of an action if such representation is false.

Laundering or Money laundering: Term used to describe investment or other transfer of money flowing from racketeering, drug transactions, and other illegal sources into legitimate channels so that its original source cannot be traced. Money laundering is a Federal Crime. Title: 18 U.S.C.A. (United States Codes Annotated) § 1956.

Motion for Summary Judgement: A summary judgement is a decision made on the basis of statements and evidence presented in the legal pleadings and documents filed, without a trial. It is used when there is no dispute as to the facts of the case, and one party is entitled to judgement as a matter of law. Summary judgement is properly granted when the evidence in support of the moving party establishes that there is no-genuine issue of material fact to be tried. A material fact is one which tends to prove or disprove an element of the claim.

The motion for summary judgement may be brought by any party to the case and supported by declarations under "oath", excerpts from depositions which are under oath, admissions of fact and other discovery, as well as case law and other legal authority, that argue that there are no triable issues of fact and that the settled facts require a summary judgement for the moving party. If the motion for summary judgement is denied, the case proceeds through the court system until settled or concluded after the trial.

Omission: The neglect to perform what the law requires. The intentional failure to act which may or may not impose criminal liability depending upon the existence, vel non, of a duty to act under the circumstances.

Plausible deniability: Plausible deniability refers to circumstances where a denial of responsibility or knowledge of wrong-doing cannot be proved as true or untrue to a lack of evidence proving the allegation. This term is often used in reference to situations where high-ranking-officials deny responsibility for or knowledge of wrong-doing by lower-ranking-officials. In certain situations officials can "plausibly-deny" any allegation, even though it may be true. It also refers to any act that leaves little or no-evidence of wrong doing or abuse.

Public servant: A public-servant is generally a person who is employed by the government, either through appointment or election. Examples include, among others, police-agents, paid and volunteer firefighters, health-agents, the public works directors and designees, city clerk and designees, code enforcement-agents, and other city personnel authorized to enforce city ordinances, statutes and codes. This also includes Executive Branch (President and his cabinet), Legislative Branch (Senators and Congressmen) and the Judicial Branch (Judges, Attorneys/Lawyers and all Court-Agents). The following is one state's definition of a public-servant: "Everyone who is a chief-executive of, or a statutory officer or employee in, a Department in the Public Service is a public servant. Contractors in a department who are not employees are not-public-employees are not public servants. For the purposes of the "Electoral Act", "public servant" is defined more broadly, notably including a person employed in the

Education-Service" as defined in the Federal, State, County or City/Municipality Sector Act.

Public service: A service that is provided by and or supported by a government or its agencies. An agency that provides a Public-service for the government or on behalf of the government.

Reasonable person: A fictional person with an ordinary degree of reason, prudence, care, foresight, or intelligence whose conduct, conclusion, or expectation in relation to a particular circumstance or fact is used as an objective standard by which to measure or determine something (as the existence of negligence) we have generally held that a reasonable person would not believe that he or she has been seized when an officer merely approaches that person in a public place and begins to ask questions.

Res: Latin. The subject matter of a trust or will. In the civil law, a thing; an object. As a term of the law, this word has a very wide and extensive signification, including not only things which are objects of property, but also such as are not capable of individual ownership. And in old English law it is said to have a general import, comprehending both corporeal and in corporeal things of whatever kind, nature, or species. By "res", according to the modern civilians, is meant everything that may form an object of rights, in opposition to "persona", which is regarded as a subject of rights. "Res", therefore, in its general meaning, comprises actions of all kinds; while in its restricted sense it comprehends every object of right, except actions. This has reference to the fundamental division of the Institutes, that all law relates either to persons, to things, or to actions.

Res is everything that may form an object of rights and includes an object, subject-matter or status. The term is particularly applied to an object, subject-matter, or status, considered as the defendant in an action, or as the object against which, directly, proceedings are taken. Thus, in a prize case, the captured vessel is "the res"; and proceedings of this character are said to be in rem. "Res" may also denote the action or proceeding, as when a cause, which is not between adversary parties, in entitled "In re _____".

Things (res) have been variously divided and classified in law, e. g., in the following ways: (1) Corporeal and in corporeal things; (2) movables and immovable; (3) res mancipi and res nec mancipi; (4) things real and things personal; (5) things in possession and choses (i. e. things) in action; (6) fungible things and things not fungible (fungibles vel non fungibles); and (7) res singulae (i. e., individual objects) and universitates rerum (i. e., aggregates of things). This is a list of res you may want to check out that may relate to "Breach of Contract" case: Res accessoria, Res adiratae; Res adjudicata; Res caduca; Res communes; Res cotroversa; Res coronae; Res corporals, Res derelict, Res fungibles; Res gestae; Res gestae witness; Res habiles; Res immobiles; Res incorporales; Res integra; Res inter alios acta; Res ipsa loquitur; Res litigosae; Res mancipi; Res mobiles; Res nova; Res nullis; Res periit domino; Res privatae; Res publicae; Res quotidianae; Res religiosae; Res universitatis.

Res Judicata: A matter adjudged; a thing judicially acted upon or decided; a thing or matter settled by judgement. Rule that a final judgement rendered by a court of competent jurisdiction on the merits is conclusive as to the rights of the parties and their privies, and, as to them, constitutes an absolute bar to a subsequent action involving the same claim, demand or cause of action. And to be applicable, requires identity in thing sued for as well as identity of cause of action, of persons and parties to action, and of quality in persons for or against whom claim is made. The sum and substance of the whole rule is that a matter once judicially decided is finally decided.

Sandbagging: Is the "tactic" used to hide or "limit" expectations of a company's or individual's-strength in order to produce greater than anticipated results.

It is a practice used by a trial attorney/lawyer who

notices, but not mentioning, a possible error during a trial in hopes of using it as a basis for appeal if the court fails to correct it. Objections must be made in a timely manner. The use of sandbagging usually does not keep the issue alive.

State bar: The State Bar Association is an association or a group of attorneys who have been admitted to practice law in a given state. However, this does not mean they have a "License to practice law", but they can bring lawsuits against those persons who engage in unauthorized practice of law.

Subjugate: To bring under control or subjection; conquer. To cause to become submissive.

Subrogation: To substitute (one person) for another. To substitute (one creditor) for another.

Subterfuge: That to which one resorts for escape or concealment.

Threat: A communicated intent to inflict physical or other harm on any person or on property. A declaration of an intention to injure another or his property by some unlawful act. A declaration of intention or determination to inflict punishment, loss, or pain on another, or to injure another or his property by the commission of some unlawful act. A menace; especially, any menace of such a nature and extent as to unsettle the mind of the person on whom it operates, and to take away from his acts that free and voluntary action which alone constitutes consent. A declaration of one's purpose or intention to work injury to the person, property, or rights of another, with a view of restraining such person's freedom of action.

The term "threat" means an avowed present determination or intent to injure presently or in the future. A statement may constitute a threat even though it is subject to a possible contingency in the maker's control. The prosecution must establish a "true threat", which means a serious threat as distinguished from words uttered as mere political argument, idle talk or jest. In determining whether words were uttered as a threat the context in which they were spoken must be considered.

Threats against the President and successors to the President, mailing of threatening communications, and other extortionate acts, are federal offenses. Title: 18 United States Codes Annotated: § 871 et seq.

Tort: (form Latin. torquere, to twist tortus, twisted, wrested aside). A private or civil wrong or injury, including action for bad faith breach of contract, for which the court will provide a remedy in the form of an action for damages. A violation of a duty imposed by general law or otherwise upon all persons occupying the relation to each other which is involved in a given transaction. There must be always a violation of some duty owing to plaintiff, and generally such duty must arise by operation of law and not by mere agreement of the parties.

A legal wrong committed upon the person or property independent of contract. It may be either (1) a direct invasion of some legal right of the individual; (2) the infraction of some public duty by which special damage accrues to the individual; (3) the violation of some private obligation by which like damage accrues to the individual.

Constitutional tort: Federal statute providing that every person who under color of any statute, ordinance, regulation, custom, or usage, of any state or territory, subjects or causes to be subjected, any citizen of the United States or any other person within the jurisdiction thereof of the deprivation of any rights, privileges, or immunities secured by the Constitution and laws, shall be liable to the party injured in an action at law, suit in equity, or other proper proceeding for redress. Title: 42; United States Codes Annotated; § 1983.

Intentional tort: Tort or wrong perpetrated by one who intends to do that which the law has declared wrong as contrasted with negligence in which the tortfeasor fails to exercise that degree of care in doing what is otherwise permissible.

Negligence: The tort or negligence consists of the existence of a legal duty owed the plaintiff by the defendant, breach of the duty, proximate causal relationship between the breach and plaintiff's injury, and damages.

Personal tort: One involving or consisting in an injury to the person or to the reputation or feelings, as distinguished from an injury or damage to real or personal property, called a "property tort".

Tortious: Wrongful; of the nature of a tort. The word "tortious" is used throughout the Restatement, Second, Torts, to denote the fact that conduct whether of act or omission is of such a character as to subject the actor to liability, under the principles of the law of torts. (§: 6); to establish "tortious act" plaintiff must prove not only existence of actionable wrong, but also that damages resulted therefrom. As used in state long-arm statutes, such as may afford a basis for jurisdiction over a nondomiciliary.

Formerly certain modes of conveyance (e. g., feoffments, fines, etc.) had the effect of passing not merely the estate of the person making the conveyance, but the whole fee-simple, to the injury of the person really entitled to the fee; and they were hence called "tortious conveyances".

Trial: A judicial examination and determination of issues between parties to action, whether they be issues of law or of fact, before a court that has jurisdiction. A judicial examination, in accordance with law of the land, of a cause, either civil or criminal, of the issues between the parties, whether of law or fact, before a court that has proper jurisdiction.

There are many types of trials: (i. e., Bifurcated trial; Civil jury trial; Examining trial; Fair and impartial trial; Mini-trial; Mistrial; Speedy trial; Trifurcated trial; Bench trial; New trial; Nonjury trial; Public trial; Separate trial; State trial; Trial at nisi prius; Trial balance; Trial by certificate; Trial by court or judge; Trial by fire; Trial by Grand Assize; Trial by jury; Summary jury trial; Trial by news media; Trial by proviso; Trial by the record; Trial by wager of battle; Trial by wager of law; Trial by witnesses; Trial court; Trial de novo; Trial jury; Trial list).

Vexatious litigation: Is a legal action or proceeding initiated maliciously and without Probable Cause by an individual who is not acting in Good Faith for the purpose of annoying or embarrassing an opponent.

The U. S. legal system permits persons to file civil-lawsuits to seek redress for injuries committed by a defendant. However, a legal action that is not likely to lead to any practical result is classified as vexatious litigation. Such litigation is regarded as frivolous and will result in the dismissal of the action by the court. A person who has been subjected to vexatious litigation may sue the plaintiff for "Malicious Prosecution", seeking damages for any costs and injuries associated with the original lawsuit.

Litigation is usually classified as vexatious when an attorney or a Pro Se Litigant (a person representing himself without an attorney) repeatedly files groundless lawsuits and repeatedly loses. Under Common Law, the frequent incitement of laws by an attorney constituted the crime of "Barratry". In common law, barratry is viewed as an archaic crime and is rarely enforced. Attorneys/Lawyers who encourage vexatious litigation are subject to discipline for violating rules of professional conduct and may be suspended from the Practice of Law or Disbarred.

Sometimes Pro Se Litigants who have lost their initial lawsuits file new actions base on the dispute contained in the original lawsuit; because the judgement of the original case is dispositive, a court will ultimately dismiss the new actions. To avoid the expenditure of court resources (blood money), as well as the costs associated with the defendant's defense of repeated frivolous claims, a court may issue an order forbidding the Pro Se Litigant to file any new actions without permission of the court.

Vexatious litigation is a type of malicious prosecution that enables the defendant/prosecution to file a tort action against the plaintiff/prosecution. A plaintiff/prosecution in a malicious prosecution must prove that legal proceeding (or multiple proceedings) was instituted by the defendant/ plaintiff, that the original proceeding was terminated in favor of the plaintiff/defendant, that there was no probable cause for the original cause for the original proceeding, and that malice, or primary purpose other than that of bringing the original action, motivated the plaintiff/ defendant. A plaintiff/defendant in such an action may recover, for example, the expenses incurred in defending the original suit or suits, as well as resulting in financial loss or injury. A plaintiff/defendant may also recover damages for mental suffering of a kind that would normally be expected to follow from the original action.

Vexatious Litigation as a noun – Filing a lawsuit with the knowledge that it has no-legal basis, with its purpose to bother, annoy, embarrass and cause legal expenses to the defendant/plaintiff. Vexatious litigation includes continuing a lawsuit after discovery of the facts shows it has absolutely no merit. Upon judgement for the defendant/plaintiff, he/she has the right to file a suit for "malicious prosecution" against the original vexatious plaintiff/defendant. Furthermore, most states allow a judge to penalize a plaintiff/defendant and his/her attorney/lawyer for filing or continuing a "frivolous" legal action with sanctions; ("Blood-Money award to the defendant/plaintiff for the trouble and or attorney/lawyer fees).

Working in concert: The definition of this statement is when the attorneys/lawyers and court officers work in together in unison against the plaintiff/defendant in collusion, coercion or threat from the judges, clerks, stenographers and all other court officers to separate you from your cause of action, evidence and split the "Blood-Money".